CELEBRITY COOKBOOK

**EDITED BY DONNA WEINERMAN
AND CAROL FERGUSON**

TELEMEDIA COMMUNICATIONS INC.

Copyright © 1994 by Telemedia Communications Inc.
TV GUIDE is a registered trademark of Telemedia Communications Inc.

All rights reserved. No part of this publication may be reproduced, stored in a retrieval system, or transmitted in any form or by any means, electronics, mechanical, photocopying, recording or otherwise, without prior permission of the publisher.

Telemedia Communications Inc.
25 Sheppard Ave. West, Suite 100, North York, Ont. M2N 6S7

Canadian Cataloguing in Publication Data
TV GUIDE Celebrity Cookbook:
Anne Murray and a galaxy of TV stars share their favorite recipes
ISBN 0-9691959-3-1
1. Cookery. I. Title: Celebrity Cookbook.
TX714.T84 1994 641.5 C94-932785-9

Cover photo of Anne Murray by Denise Grant
Food photography: Michael Waring
Illustrations: Martha Newbigging

Cookbook Editor: Donna Weinerman
Food Editor: Carol Ferguson
Art Director: Toba Krasman-Lakier
Design: Diane Scally
Copy Editor: Barbara Kelly
Photo Researcher: Sara Penttila
Editorial Coordinator: Erin McLaughlin
Contributing Writers: Bill Brioux, C. Lee Crawford, Glenn Esterly, Jennifer Fisher, Seli Groves, Joan P. Hunt, Kelly Lamb, Michael Logan, Jane Marion, Bill Marsano, Lee Anne Nicholson, Mike Norris, Donna Paris, John Porteous, Andrew Ryan, Bonnie Siegler, Tracey Williams, Les Wiseman

TV GUIDE Editor: Nicholas Hirst
Group Vice-President and Publisher: Graham Morris
Associate Publisher: Naomi Judith Rose
Vice-President, Circulation: Gloria MacDonald
Production Manager: Cathy Pettit
Assistant Production Manager: Daryl Way

Produced and printed in Canada

Distributed by Firefly Books

PREFACE

When TV GUIDE first introduced the Celebrity Chef feature on January 16, 1982 – veteran news anchor Harvey Kirck talked about his diet plan being at odds with his love of rich food – little did we know that it would become one of the most popular features in the magazine.

Since then, TV GUIDE has collected more than 600 recipes from television stars past and present. And if there's one thing they all have in common, the stars *love* their food. Lucky for us, they also love to share their favorite recipes and, often, the memories that go with them. Anne Murray, for one, shares her mom's recipe for Cherry Cake, a traditional Maritime specialty.

Some of the recipes come from the kitchens of celebrity-owned restaurants including Wayne Gretzky's and Michael Jordan's, while others come from the kitchens of restaurants featured on a TV series, such as the Bull & Finch Pub made famous by *Cheers*. Several shows have even inspired their own cookbooks, from *Northern Exposure* to *Regis & Kathie Lee*.

There are recipes for every holiday season, too. Among guaranteed crowd pleasers: Rita MacNeil's Molasses Cookies for Christmas, Geraldo Rivera's Potato Pancakes for Hanukkah, and Martha Stewart's Easter Ham.

While our weekly Celebrity Chef recipes are undoubtedly mouth-watering, the stories have also been eye-opening. *Picket Fences* star Kathy Baker could easily have been a gourmet chef – she graduated from the renowned Paris Cordon Bleu. *Play-Along*'s Shari Lewis confesses she often cooks lamb (sorry, Lamb Chop).

Who's minding the kitchen? We are at TV GUIDE. We've been doing it for the past 12 years, and we'll continue doing so every week. Happy cooking!

CONTENTS

HOSTS	All that talking helps work up an appetite	4
NEWS	Getting the scoop on incredible edibles	28
DRAMA	Star grazing on heavenly fare off the air	38
COMEDY	Funny folk get serious about their food	58
SOAPS	Off the air, soap stars are really cookin', too	82
CHEFS	Masters of the kitchen share recipes for success	92
SPORTS	Scoring high points with culinary inspiration	102
MUSIC	If music be the food of love, read on	116
INDEX		127

HOSTS All that talking helps work up an appetite

Oprah Winfrey trims the fat with her un-fried chicken

Like most of us, talk-show superstar Oprah Winfrey believed that healthy eating meant sacrificing taste – until she met chef Rosie Daley, creator of the culinary technique of "un-frying."

"Rosie has perfected un-frying my favorites like chicken and catfish – meaning that chicken is not fried, but tastes like it is," says Winfrey. "You can use the same process for anything else you choose to un-fry. We have served un-fried chicken to guests, and they thought it was the best fried chicken they ever had."

Three years and 72 pounds ago, Winfrey was introduced to Daley's cooking at the Cal-a-Vie spa in Vista, Calif. After tasting her delicious meals, Winfrey persuaded Daley to move from the spa to Chicago and become her personal chef.

Now Daley's cookbook, "In the Kitchen with Rosie" (Knopf, 1994), is a best-seller across North America. This recipe is adapted from the book.

UN-FRIED CHICKEN

6	chicken drumsticks	6
6	chicken breast halves	6
3-1/2 cups	ice water	875 mL
1 cup	plain nonfat yogurt	250 mL
	Vegetable oil	
BREADING		
1 cup	dried Italian bread crumbs	250 mL
1 cup	all-purpose flour	250 mL
1 tbsp	Old Bay seasoning	15 mL
1/2 tsp	each: garlic powder, thyme, basil, oregano	2 mL
1/8 tsp	black pepper	.5 mL

Remove skin from chicken. Place chicken in large bowl with ice water. Put yogurt into medium bowl. Set aside. Spray a baking sheet with vegetable oil. BREADING: Combine all ingredients in large tight-sealing bag; shake to mix. Remove 2 pieces of chicken from ice water. Roll each piece in yogurt. Put chicken into plastic bag, seal and shake, coating thoroughly. Transfer breaded chicken to oiled baking sheet. Repeat until all 12 pieces are breaded. Spray chicken lightly with vegetable oil. Place baking sheet on bottom shelf of 400°F (200°C) oven and bake for 1 hour, turning pieces every 20 minutes for even browning. Serve hot or at room temperature. Makes about 6 servings.

PHOTO: MICHEAL P. MCLAUGHLIN

 **HOSTS**

Shirley Solomon's passion for food is rolled up in her past

"I just can't relate to those people who go to a great restaurant and order a salad and a glass of water. They seem so passionless." So says Shirley Solomon, host of CTV's daily current-affairs talk show *Shirley*.

Solomon's theories on dining stem from her personal views on eating well and on her theory about people who love good food: "They just seem to enjoy life more. They're more interesting."

When taping *Shirley*, Solomon often eats out, but when she finds the time, she loves cooking a meal for her family (husband Les and daughter Stephanie). She cooks things like pasta, chicken and fish because "they're simple to prepare and taste good."

A native of Germany who immigrated to Canada when she was a child, Solomon also likes to prepare traditional dishes from her childhood: "I like hearty food like my mother always used to make – like Cabbage Rolls."

CABBAGE ROLLS

1 lb	lean ground beef	500 g
1/4 cup	uncooked rice	50 mL
1	egg	1
1	onion, grated	1
1/4 tsp	salt	1 mL
12	cabbage leaves	12
1	can (28 oz/796 mL) tomatoes	1
1	can (19 oz/540 mL) tomato juice	1
1/4 cup	lemon juice	50 mL
1/2 cup	brown sugar	125 mL

Mix together ground beef, rice, egg, onion and salt. Blanch cabbage leaves by covering with boiling water for 2 to 3 minutes; drain. Place spoonful of meat mixture in each leaf and roll up, tucking in ends. Place rolls close together in Dutch oven. Combine tomatoes, tomato juice, lemon juice and brown sugar. Pour over cabbage rolls, adding water to cover if necessary. Cover and cook over medium heat for 30 minutes. Reduce heat and simmer slowly for about 20 minutes. Uncover and bake in 350°F (180°C) oven for 20 minutes. Add more hot water if needed during baking. Makes about 12 cabbage rolls.

HOSTS

Geraldo Rivera spices up life and latkes with a dash of hot sauce

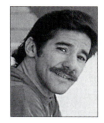

Geraldo Rivera recalls that when he was a kid both halves of his ethnic background were represented at the family table.

"There were times when we'd have the most ecumenical mixture of dishes," remembers Rivera, whose mother, Lily, is Jewish and whose father, Cruz, was Puerto Rican. "Christmas and Hanukkah were invariably grand holidays in my family. The Hispanic relatives would bring rice and beans, and the Jewish relatives would bring potato pancakes."

Unfortunately, Rivera's hectic schedule as host of the weekday talk show doesn't leave him as much time as he'd like for concocting in the kitchen. "I'm an event cook," he says. "I save my cooking for birthdays or family reunions. And there were 21 kids in my father's family alone, so you can imagine how big our family reunions are."

And while Rivera's recipe for Potato Pancakes is a tradition for Hanukkah, he quickly brings out the salsa and sour cream when his Hispanic relatives drop over. "As with life," he sums up, "on all my food, I like to add hot sauce."

POTATO PANCAKES (LATKES)

5	baking potatoes (2-1/2 lbs/1.25 kg)	5
2	small onions, quartered	2
3	eggs	3
3 tbsp	all-purpose flour	50 mL
3/4 tsp	salt	4 mL
1/4 tsp	pepper	1 mL
	Vegetable oil	
	Sour cream, applesauce or salsa	

Peel potatoes. By hand or in food processor using shredder blade, alternately shred potatoes and onions. Transfer mixture to colander. With hands, squeeze out as much moisture as possible and discard liquid. Transfer mixture to large bowl. Mix in eggs, flour, salt and pepper. Let stand for 5 minutes. Pour out any liquid. In large skillet, heat 1/4 inch (5 mm) oil over high heat until hot but not smoking. For each pancake, spoon 1/4 cup (50 mL) of mixture into skillet, leaving about 1 inch (3 cm) between each. Flatten slightly with spoon. Fry for 3 minutes or until well browned and crisp around edges. With slotted spatula, turn pancakes over and fry for 2 to 3 minutes longer or until crisp and golden brown. Transfer to paper towel and drain well. Repeat with remaining mixture, removing cooked bits from skillet and adding more oil when necessary. Serve with applesauce, sour cream or salsa. Makes 4 to 6 servings.

PHOTO: WYATT COUNTS/OUTLINE PRESS

 **HOSTS**

Dini Petty gets cracking on the weekend for Pete's sake

Of all the recipes she's introduced on *The Dini Petty Show* over the years, Dini Petty gets more requests for "Pete's Sauce" than anything else. "It's named for Pete, my better half, who loves to barbecue," says Petty. "We just mix together one-half cup of ketchup, one-third cup each of mustard and relish, two tablespoons of HP sauce and a teaspoon of Worcestershire sauce; it's great on hamburgers."

But during the week when she's busy hosting her daily talk show, the mother of two admits she seldom has time to cook.

So she relies on her valued housekeeper, Belma, whom she describes as a "one-woman catering service; I always introduce her as my wife."

One recipe that has become a favorite is bananas flambé served over ice cream, a recipe from Bonnie Stern who's often featured on Petty's show. And what about the calories? "I've always been a very athletic person. I was a tomboy when I was a kid, so I always just ate." Another favorite is Eggs Goldenrod, which she prepares for Sunday brunch at her country home north of Toronto.

EGGS GOLDENROD

2 tbsp	butter	25 mL
2 tbsp	all-purpose flour	25 mL
2 cups	milk	500 mL
1 cup	shredded old cheddar cheese	250 mL
	Salt and pepper to taste	
8	hard-cooked eggs	8
4	English muffins, split and toasted	4
8	slices peameal bacon (optional)	8

In heavy saucepan, melt butter over medium heat. Stir in flour and cook for 2 to 3 minutes. Stir in milk; cook, stirring, until thickened. Add cheese and stir until melted. Season with salt and pepper. Separate egg yolks and whites. Chop whites and add to cheese sauce. Place a slice of bacon (if using) on each muffin half. Top with cheese sauce mixture. Sprinkle with crumbled egg yolks. Makes 4 servings.

HOSTS

Jenny Jones trades girls' night out for cooking at home

Jenny Jones, host of the syndicated *Jenny Jones Show*, is one of those rare people who'd prefer to cook any time rather than go to a restaurant.

"I ate out in restaurants for so many years while on the road that it'll last me a lifetime," says Jones. After high school, Jones toured with rock bands as a drummer, singer and comedienne. She landed in Las Vegas with her all-girl band, and became Wayne Newton's backup. She was on the comedy circuit for five years, then on the road with her for-women-only "Girls' Night Out" concerts.

The former Janina Stronski grew up in London, Ont. "We ate potatoes, cabbage rolls and sausage, which I still like. But now, when she cooks she often makes Carrot-Bran Muffins. "I got the idea from a muffin place in Toronto. They taste great but are low in sugar and fat."

CARROT-BRAN MUFFINS

1-1/2 cups	unbleached all-purpose flour	375 mL
1/2 cup	whole wheat flour	125 mL
2 tsp	baking powder	10 mL
1 tsp	baking soda	5 mL
1 tsp	cinnamon	5 mL
1/3 cup	granulated sugar	75 mL
1 cup	wheat bran	250 mL
2	eggs, beaten	2
3/4 cup	skim milk	175 mL
1/4 cup	canola oil	50 mL
1 cup	grated carrots	250 mL
1/2 cup	drained crushed pineapple	125 mL
3/4 tsp	vanilla	4 mL
1 cup	chopped walnuts	250 mL

In large bowl, mix together flours, baking powder, baking soda, cinnamon and sugar. Stir in bran. Combine eggs, milk, oil, carrots, pineapple and vanilla. Add to dry ingredients, gently mixing just until moistened. Fold in nuts. Spoon into paper-lined or greased muffin tins. Bake in 400°F (200°C) oven for about 20 minutes or until muffins test done. Makes 12 muffins.

PHOTO: DANA FINEMAN/SYGMA

HOSTS

Kathie Lee Gifford's grilling techniques keep her out of the kitchen

One of the most popular segments of the daytime talk show *Live with Regis & Kathie Lee* has always been the cooking demonstrations, so it was a natural for Regis Philbin and Kathie Lee Gifford to publish a collection of their favorite recipes in "Cooking with Regis & Kathie Lee" (Hyperion, 1993).

Barbecuing becomes the favorite method of cooking at the Gifford's Connecticut home during the summer, with Philbin and his wife, Joy, as frequent dinner guests.

Since his health problems last year, Philbin is trying to stay away from the traditional barbecue items of hot dogs and hamburgers. And what is Kathie Lee staying away from – the kitchen! Laughs Gifford: "I want to ride horses. I want to play tennis."

SEAFOOD SHISH KEBABS

TEQUILA-LIME MARINADE

1/4 cup	tequila	50 mL
1 tbsp	chopped fresh cilantro	15 mL
	Juice of 2 limes	
1 tsp	finely chopped fresh herbs	5 mL

SEAFOOD KEBABS

1/2 lb	each: medium shrimp, salmon and tuna fillets, swordfish	250 g
2	each: onions, red and yellow peppers	2

HOT AND HONEY SAUCE

1/2 cup	hot sauce	125 mL
1/4 cup	honey	50 mL
3 tbsp	butter, melted	50 mL
1 tbsp	white vinegar	15 mL
1 tsp	Tabasco sauce	5 mL
1 tsp	minced garlic	5 mL
1/4 tsp	celery salt	1 mL

MARINADE: In shallow glass dish, combine marinade ingredients. KEBABS: Peel and devein shrimp. Cut fish and vegetables into 1-inch (3 cm) pieces. Thread alternately onto 8 skewers. Place in marinade, cover and refrigerate for 2 hours. SAUCE: Stir ingredients together. Brush grill with oil; preheat barbecue. Remove kebabs from marinade and place on grill. Cook for 5 to 7 minutes or until fish is just cooked through, turning frequently. Serve with sauce. Makes 8 servings.

HOSTS

Shari Lewis gives voice to her love of lamb and other delights

Shari Lewis introduced her beloved puppet Lamb Chop in 1957 on *Captain Kangaroo*. Since then, the two have remained a fixture in children's television. It is with some hesitation, then, that Lewis confides, "I love lamb. It horrifies everybody. Even as we speak, I have Yorkshire lamb pot cooking."

The 60-year-old creator and host of *Lamb Chop's Play-Along* laughs as she relates this. Clearly her intent is not to offend, but Lewis is enthusiastic about food. "I love to eat. *That* is the great motivation for cooking."

Lewis has applied this same enthusiasm to all aspects of her career. Born in New York, the award-winning performer earned her first TV credits in Toronto, appearing on CBC's *Robert Goulet Show*. It was also on TV that she first learned to cook. "I was working in New York on *Hi Mom*. The chef on the show taught me to cook on air." Lewis adapted her recipe for Mozzarella Marinara from one she took from a chef in a California restaurant.

PHOTO: ERIC RASMUSSEN/OUTLINE PRESS

MOZZARELLA MARINARA

1 lb	mozzarella cheese, sliced into 1/2-inch (1 cm) slabs	500 g
2	eggs, lightly beaten	2
1/2 cup	all-purpose flour	125 mL
1 cup	bread crumbs (herb-seasoned)	250 mL
	Olive oil	
1-1/4 cups	pizza sauce	300 mL
1 can	flat anchovies (about 1.75 oz/50 g)	1

Dip each slice of cheese into egg, then flour, back into egg and then into bread crumbs. Pack bread crumbs against surface of cheese so it forms a good crust. Place slices on plate and freeze for 20 minutes or refrigerate for 1 hour. In skillet, heat 1/4 inch (5 mm) oil until very hot. Place cold cheese slices into oil and allow them to brown crisply on each side. When cheese is just beginning to ooze through the crust, carefully lift slices out of pan. Place on paper towels to drain. Meanwhile, heat pizza sauce in small saucepan. On each serving plate, place large tablespoon of sauce; top with 1 or 2 slices of fried cheese, another tablespoon of sauce and a strip of anchovy. Makes 4 to 6 servings.

HOSTS

Artful **David Gilmour** avoids culinary clichés with a garlic surprise

When David Gilmour, CBC *Prime Time News* movie reviewer and host of Newsworld's *On the Arts with David Gilmour* conducts an interview, he has no set recipe for his conversations: "I want guests to be free to talk about things they don't usually discuss," he says. But from his previous experience as host of the *Journal Friday Night*, he knows that a key ingredient to any good interview is the element of surprise.

"Ask clichéd questions and you get clichéd answers," he says. "You have to get at what the guest *really* wants to talk about – like how they cooked up all those wonderful cinematic moments."

Gilmour cooks up his own special moments when he heads for the kitchen. One of his favorites is Garlic Chicken Ragout – a recipe that includes 50 cloves of garlic, which he says only *sounds* like a garlic overload. Gilmour says, "It actually tastes wonderful!"

GARLIC CHICKEN RAGOUT

8	chicken legs	8
1/4 cup	olive oil	50 mL
50	cloves garlic, unpeeled	50
1-1/2 cups	dry white wine	375 mL
1/2 cup	chicken stock	125 mL
1 tsp	salt	5 mL
1 tsp	black pepper	5 mL
1/2 tsp	ground allspice	2 mL
1/4 tsp	cinnamon	1 mL
2 tbsp	chopped fresh tarragon	25 mL
1/2 cup	chopped fresh parsley	125 mL
1/2 cup	chopped celery leaves	125 mL

Cut chicken legs into thighs and drumsticks. In large skillet, heat oil and brown chicken pieces on all sides. Add garlic cloves and brown very lightly. Drain off excess fat. Transfer chicken and garlic to baking dish. Rub with oil and place in baking pan. Sprinkle with garlic cloves. Combine remaining ingredients and pour over chicken. Cover and bake in 375°F (190°C) oven for 1 hour or until tender. Remove garlic cloves. Squeeze out the garlic, discarding skin. Mash garlic to purée and serve with the chicken. Serve with steamed new potatoes. Makes 8 servings.

HOSTS

What's a traditional French-Canadian dish that scores big with **Alex Trebek**?

Say you're a contestant on *Jeopardy!* and this answer comes up: French-Canadian Tourtière. The only person likely to score points is the host himself. The correct answer is: What is Alex Trebek's all-time favorite Christmas dish? The recipe is a traditional one the game-show host learned from his French-Canadian mother. "I grew up in Sudbury on a basic Northern Ontario meat-and-potatoes diet," he says.

"My father was a chef, but he didn't cook at home. Mom was a great cook and did all the cooking for the family."

Trebek has been cooking since he was 12, and these days he cooks for guests at home whenever he gets the chance. "You can dazzle people with fairly simple dishes," he says. "The secret is not to be afraid to experiment."

Come the Yuletide season, visitors to Trebek's Los Angeles home are likely to sample his Tourtière. "I remember we used to have it after midnight mass on Christmas Eve and all through the holidays. It was a tradition." A tradition, we assume, he's not about to jeopardize.

TOURTIÈRE TREBEK

1 lb	ground pork	500 g
3/4 lb	ground veal	375 g
1	large onion, chopped	1
1 tsp	poultry seasoning	5 mL
1/2 tsp	thyme	2 mL
1/4 tsp	ground clove	1 mL
1/4 cup	red wine, beef stock or water	50 mL
1/2 cup	fresh bread crumbs	125 mL
	Salt and pepper	
	Pastry for double-crust pie (9 inch/23 cm)	
	Milk or lightly beaten egg	

In large pan, combine meat, onions, seasonings and wine; cook over low heat for 1 hour. Drain fat. Stir in bread crumbs, and salt and pepper to taste. Let cool for about 45 minutes. Roll out pastry and line a 9-inch (23 cm) pie plate. Spoon in filling; cover with pastry. Cut steam vents in top and seal edges. Brush top lightly with milk or egg. Bake in 350°F (180°C) oven for 1 hour or until pastry is golden brown. Makes 4 to 6 servings.

HOSTS

Robin Leach dishes the eating styles of the oh so rich and famous

When he set out to write "The Lifestyles of the Rich and Famous Cookbook" (Viking Studio Books, 1992), Robin Leach was surprised by what he learned.

"The first time I went to Joan Collins' house, I had this vision of opening a fridge overflowing with champagne and caviar. What I found was one lonely can of baked beans." Roger Moore was another surprise. "Roger is a gourmet cook, but what was it he wanted us to have in the book? His recipe for scrambled eggs!"

Leach finds time to prepare an occasional meal at his Connecticut home. "I really do spend far too much time eating out and at parties," he says.

As well as sharing favorite recipes from celebrities such as Ivana Trump and Elizabeth Taylor, Leach included his Rich and Famous Chicken recipe in his book. "One of the essential ingredients is champagne – a whole bottle goes into the pot. If that seems a bit excessive, save the Cristal for another occasion and add a bottle of less expensive bubbly."

RICH AND FAMOUS CHICKEN

3 lb	chicken pieces	1.5 kg
	Worcestershire sauce	
	Dry mustard	
	Fresh lemon juice	
2	onions, sliced	2
4 cups	champagne	1 L
1/4 cup	butter	50 mL
1	can each: petit pois and baby carrots, drained (10 oz/284 mL)*	1
1	can cream of mushroom soup (10 oz/284 mL)	1
4	potatoes, halved	4
	Basil, oregano, black pepper	

* Any vegetables may be substituted

Season chicken with Worcestershire sauce, mustard and lemon juice. Spread onions over bottom of roasting pan; drizzle with champagne. Place chicken pieces on top; dot with half of butter; pour in more champagne. Cover with peas; sprinkle lightly with herbs and pepper. Place carrots on top; dot with butter; sprinkle with more herbs and pepper; drizzle with champagne. Spread soup over all. Place halved potatoes into soup-covered vegetables, leaving top half exposed. Pour in enough champagne to cover vegetables. Cover and bake in 425°F (220°C) oven for 1 hour. Uncover and bake for 15 minutes longer to brown potatoes. Serves 6.

HOSTS

Entertaining **John Tesh** plays second fiddle in the kitchen

In his bachelor days, John Tesh – co-host with Mary Hart of *Entertainment Tonight* – cooked more out of necessity than pleasure. "I'd mainly cook pasta dishes," recalls Tesh, whose one specialty was Stuffed Peppers with Eggplant and Feta Cheese. Now that he's married to actress and gourmet cook Connie Sellecca, he has been more than happy to throw in the towel.

Sellecca's mouth-watering Italian cooking is taken straight from the pages of an unpublished collection of her family's secret Old World Italian recipes. But she doesn't cook and tell. "Connie guards with her life this old, tattered, grey family cookbook with a photocopy of Grandma Sellecca on the cover," laughs Tesh.

After Sellecca – and her cooking – Tesh's first love is composing. The Emmy Award-winning musician, who began playing the piano at age six, wrote the theme song to the 1992 Olympics and came out with his seventh instrumental album in 1993. "Monterey Nights" was inspired by the breezy November evening when Tesh asked Sellecca for her hand in marriage.

PHOTO: EDDIE ADAMS/SYGMA

STUFFED PEPPERS WITH EGGPLANT AND FETA CHEESE

6	medium-sized green peppers	6
4 cups	cooked brown rice	1 L
1 cup	diced cooked eggplant	250 mL
1-1/2 tbsp	chopped fresh basil	20 mL
1 tbsp	extra virgin olive oil	15 mL
4	plum tomatoes, diced	4
	Salt and pepper to taste	
1/2 cup	crumbled feta cheese	125 mL
1/4 cup	pitted black olives, minced	50 mL

Cut tops off peppers and remove seeds. In bowl, combine rice, eggplant, basil, olive oil, tomatoes, salt and pepper. Stuff peppers with mixture. Place peppers in well-oiled casserole dish. Spray top of peppers with water. Cover and bake in 350°F (180°C) oven for 30 minutes or until peppers are tender. Top with feta cheese and minced olives. Makes 6 servings.

HOSTS

Wayne Rostad is on the road again with simple down-home fare

If you're ever out Wayne Rostad's way, be sure to drop in for dinner. Odds are you'll get a hearty meal of meat and potatoes or the house specialty, Rostad Goulash. "I had macaroni a thousand different ways when I was a kid, and I still like it better than steak," says the host of CBC's *On the Road Again*.

The country singer-TV host has invented a lot of unusual macaroni dishes over the years, but when his son, Josh, made a repeat request for his Rostad Goulash, "I knew I had finally created a macaroni hit."

The family menu also includes a lot of vegetable dishes prepared with fresh produce from their farm in the Ottawa Valley. "Often everything on the dinner table is from our farm. It's a good down-home feeling that we enjoy."

Rostad's ability to re-create that down-home feeling on air led to the nationally popular *On the Road Again*. "I love the show," says Rostad. "I get to travel and meet everyday, next-door-neighbor kind of people. Then I get to come home and dine out on the stories for weeks afterward."

ROSTAD GOULASH

1 lb	ground beef	500 g
1 tbsp	vegetable oil	15 mL
1	large onion, chopped	1
1	large green pepper, chopped	1
2 cups	sliced celery	500 mL
1 lb	elbow macaroni	500 g
3 cups	stewed tomatoes, with juice	750 mL
1/4 tsp	Worcestershire sauce	1 mL
1 tsp	HP sauce	5 mL
1/2 tsp	salt	2 mL
1/4 tsp	pepper	1 mL
	Coarse bread crumbs	

In large skillet, brown ground beef. Drain fat; remove beef and set aside. Add oil to skillet. Add onion, pepper and celery; cook until softened. Meanwhile, in large pot of boiling salted water, cook macaroni until tender but firm; drain. In large greased casserole, combine all ingredients. Sprinkle with bread crumbs. Bake in 350°F (180°C) oven for 15 minutes or until bubbling hot. Serve with Caesar salad and garlic bread if desired. Makes 4 to 6 servings.

HOSTS

Rockin' **Dick Clark** rolls back time in his restaurant-sized kitchen

For more than 22 years, Dick Clark has been counting down the New Year on *Dick Clark's New Year's Rockin' Eve*. But the man who helped launch the rock revolution with *American Bandstand* in the '50s swears he had no intention of becoming an "Auld Lang Syne" tradition. "I only took the job temporarily because we didn't have a host for Times Square in New York," says Clark.

While viewers party at home, Clark and his crew pack up after midnight and head for his favorite Manhattan eatery, P.J. Clarke's, where they tuck into burgers and beer and watch the rest of the show.

Things are different back home in Malibu where Clark and wife Kari make full use of their restaurant-sized kitchen complete with brick pizza oven. The professional equipment and well-stocked pantry allow plenty of room to experiment, and that's exactly the way Clark developed his Cajun Corn Chowder. He first tasted this original soup at an L.A. eatery, quizzed the chef about the ingredients, then went home and "added and subtracted things. It's not creamy, it's light – and just as hot and spicy as you want to make it."

CAJUN CORN CHOWDER

2-1/4 cups	skim milk	550 mL
1-3/4 cups	chicken broth	425 mL
1	can (12 oz/370 g) corn kernels with chopped peppers	1
1 cup	frozen corn kernels	250 mL
1	small sweet pepper, diced	1
	Celery seed, cayenne pepper, paprika, garlic powder, onion powder, coarse black pepper, marjoram	
1 cup	chopped onion	250 mL
1 cup	chopped celery	250 mL
2 tbsp	margarine	25 mL

In large saucepan, combine milk, chicken broth, canned corn, frozen corn and diced pepper. Shake in spices to taste. In another pan, sauté onions and celery in margarine; add to corn mixture. Simmer for 10 to 15 minutes, then let stand for 1 to 2 hours. Reheat and serve. Makes about 6 servings.

PHOTO: E.J. CAMP/OUTLINE PRESS

 **HOSTS**

Flying gourmet **Robert Scully** ventures into devilish drinks and appetizers

Hosting CBC's *Venture* as well as Radio-Canada's French-language *Scully Rencontre* keeps multilingual Robert Scully (he speaks Spanish, German, French and English) shuttling continuously between Toronto, Montreal, Paris and New York – a schedule that makes him "more of a flying gourmet than a galloping one."

From Paris comes his culinary invention, Parc Montsouris, named in honor of his favorite park in the French capital. "One day, I was making devilled eggs and planted some sprigs of parsley in each of them. I noticed if you pack the eggs closely together on the plate, it really does look like a park full of trees."

For New Year's Eve or other special occasions, the eggs with their foie gras filling make a perfect accompaniment to another aptly named Scully creation, the Devil's Advocate Cocktail. "I've experimented before, but this one is the smoothest, the strongest, the most convincing – which is why it has this name."

Adds Scully, "It goes down smoothly and does wonders for the morale." Cheers and bon appetit!

DEVIL'S ADVOCATE COCKTAIL

1/2 oz	each: Cointreau, cognac, scotch, vodka, gin, white rum	15 mL
2 oz	each: orange juice, water	60 mL
Dash	gumbo filé and/or pepper	Dash

Pour all 6 liquors into large glass, beginning with the colored and ending with the white. Add orange juice and stir. Add water and stir again. Add dash of gumbo filé and/or pepper, stirring one last time. Makes a double.

PARC MONTSOURIS

12	hard-cooked eggs	12
6 oz	foie gras	175 g
72	sprigs fresh parsley	72

Cut eggs in half lengthwise. Scoop out yolks and mix with foie gras. Spoon mixture back into egg whites and pack tightly. Plant sprigs of parsley (3 per egg) upright in yolk mixture. On serving platter, place eggs close together to create park-like appearance. Makes 24.

HOSTS

For **Eric Malling**, the focus is on family and traditional Scandinavian dishes

The host of CTV's *W5 with Eric Malling* comes by his good taste naturally. With a Swedish mother and Danish father, Eric Malling was raised in a home where food was central to family life and eating was an important ritual.

"There was always something pickling in a crock or the smoky smell of something curing." His father was a butcher, and Malling's Meat Market was a gathering place in Swift Current, Sask. where he grew up.

Today, in Toronto, life in the Malling household still revolves around traditional food. Malling considers dinner an important family event with everyone involved in the preparation. Christmas, especially, is the reserve of his heritage. The focal point is a fabulous smorgasbord that includes herring, gravlax and his Swedish Meatballs.

SWEDISH MEATBALLS

1/4 cup	butter	50 mL
1/3 cup	finely chopped onion	75 mL
1	egg, beaten	1
1/2 cup	milk	125 mL
1/4 cup	dried bread crumbs	50 mL
2 tsp	granulated sugar	10 mL
1-1/2 tsp	salt	7 mL
1 tsp	each: allspice, nutmeg	5 mL
1/2 tsp	dry mustard	2 mL
1-1/2 lbs	lean ground beef	750 g
1/2 cup	all-purpose flour	125 mL
SAUCE		
2 tbsp	butter	25 mL
1 cup	milk	250 mL
3/4 cup	whipping cream	175 mL
1 tsp	granulated sugar	5 mL
1/2 tsp	each: allspice, nutmeg, dry mustard, salt	2 mL
Pinch	freshly ground pepper	Pinch

In skillet, heat half of butter. Add onion and cook until tender. In bowl, stir in egg, milk, bread crumbs, sugar, salt and spices. Let stand 3 minutes. Add beef and onions; mix well. Form into tiny meatballs and roll in flour. In skillet, heat remaining butter. Brown meatballs; remove and keep warm. SAUCE: In same skillet, melt butter and stir in remaining ingredients. Return meatballs to skillet and cook over low heat, stirring occasionally, for 10 minutes. (Sauce will thicken.) Serves 4 to 6.

HOSTS

Regis Philbin scares up a sweet treat for Halloween

Regis Philbin doesn't scare easily. On camera each weekday as co-host of *Live with Regis & Kathie Lee*, he's seldom caught off guard. And at home in his New York apartment, Philbin remains fearless – even at Halloween. When scary little trick-or-treaters come to his door, he's become famous for donning a horrible face mask to scare the daylights out of *them*!

However, Philbin did get a *real* scare, when an emergency angioplasty forced him to take a hard look at his diet. "I cut down on a lot of the fat content in foods," he says. But even the fit and feisty enjoy a rich-tasting dessert occasionally. This light Pumpkin Cheesecake is much lower in fat than most and is the perfect treat anytime. The recipe is from the daytime duo's second cookbook, "Entertaining with Regis & Kathie Lee" (Hyperion, 1994).

PHOTO: PAT HARBRON/OUTLINE PRESS

PUMPKIN CHEESECAKE

7	egg whites, at room temperature	7
2	egg yolks	2
1-1/2 lbs	ricotta cheese	750 g
1 cup	granulated sugar	250 mL
1-1/2 cups	puréed, cooked or canned pumpkin	375 mL
1-1/2 tsp	vanilla extract	7 mL
1 tsp	pumpkin pie spice	5 mL
1 tsp	baking powder	5 mL
	Icing sugar or whipped cream	

Butter an 8-inch (23 cm) springform pan. Dust with flour and tap out excess. Using electric mixer, beat egg whites until they form stiff, shiny peaks. In another bowl, using the same beaters, beat together egg yolks, ricotta, sugar, pumpkin, vanilla, spice and baking powder just until smooth. Using rubber spatula, fold in egg whites just until combined. Turn batter into prepared pan. Bake in 350°F (180°C) oven for 75 to 85 minutes or until cake tester inserted in centre comes out clean. Place cake on wire rack and let cool completely. Cover cake with plastic wrap and refrigerate for at least 6 hours or until cold. To serve, remove from pan and dust top of cake with icing sugar or decorate with whipped cream. Makes 8 to 12 servings.

HOSTS

Chocoholic **Lynette Jennings** is at home with designer food

Most of us know Lynette Jennings as the affable host of *Lynette Jennings Home*, on CBC's renovation and home-decorating show. What most of us don't know about the Illinois native is that she's an avowed chocoholic. Jennings comes by her delicious habit naturally: Her grandmother was a professional chocolatier.

Jenning's interest in food, however, encompasses more than just chocolate. She loves "hearty food, chili and things that cowboys might like." That includes plenty of barbecuing since she installed an indoor gas grill in her midtown Toronto home.

She also enjoys presenting food in an attractive manner. "I have no patience for everyday cooking. What I like to do on the *Home* food segments is presentation rather than preparation. For instance, I'll make a birthday cake from a box rather than from scratch and then do some spectacular decoration. I try to present food in an unusual way because I feel that's half the fun of eating. Designer food is what I call it."

CHOCOLATE TURTLE SQUARES

BASE
1-3/4 cups	all-purpose flour	425 mL
1 cup	granulated sugar	250 mL
1/3 cup	unsweetened cocoa powder	75 mL
1/2 cup	soft butter	125 mL

TOPPING
1-1/2 cups	pecan halves	375 mL
1/2 cup	brown sugar	125 mL
2/3 cup	soft butter	150 mL
3/4 cup	chocolate chips	175 mL

BASE: In food processor, combine flour, sugar, cocoa and butter. Process until blended. Press into ungreased 13 x 9-inch (3.5 L) baking pan. TOPPING: Arrange pecan halves, flat side down, evenly over base. In small saucepan, combine brown sugar and butter. Cook over medium heat, stirring, until mixture comes to boil. Boil for 1 minute, stirring constantly. Pour mixture evenly over pecans. Bake in 350°F (180°C) oven for about 20 minutes or until topping is bubbly. Remove from oven and immediately sprinkle chocolate chips on top; do not spread. Let cool. Cut into small squares. Makes about 40 pieces.

HOSTS

Rock reporter **Monika Deol** will try anything – especially if it's spicy and hot

When it comes to food "the hotter the better," says *MuchMusic*'s rock reporter Monika Deol. Born in India, Deol was raised in Beausejour, Man. before moving to Toronto's CITY-TV and *MuchMusic*. She brought with her a fondness for traditional Indian food. "My parents were both excellent cooks."

Excellence in cooking is not a trait Deol has mastered yet, but she does admit to "a terrific appetite. I'll try anything – French, Russian, Thai – especially if it's spicy and hot *hot*." She also has a weakness for "chocolate anything" – not that it shows. She keeps in shape by avoiding junk food and walking a lot, and by juggling several TV jobs – she also handles entertainment news assignments at CITY-TV and hosts the *Electric Circus* dance party.

When Deol does find time to relax, she likes to prepare romantic dinners for someone special. Atmosphere is important. That includes candles, music and, of course, spicy Indian delicacies. Chicken Biryani is a favorite lure of hers.

CHICKEN BIRYANI

2	large chicken breasts	2
2 cups	water	500 mL
1/2 tsp	cumin seeds	2 mL
1/2 tsp	salt	2 mL
1	whole clove	1
1	brown cardamom pod	1
1	large onion, chopped	1
1 tbsp	oil or clarified butter	15 mL
1/2 cup	whole blanched almonds	125 mL
1/3 cup	raisins	75 mL
1/2 tsp	chili powder	2 mL
1 cup	basmati or long grain rice	250 mL
1	tomato, chopped	1

Skin and bone chicken breasts; cut into cubes. In saucepan, combine chicken, water, cumin seeds, salt, clove and cardamom. Bring to boil and simmer until tender. Set broth and chicken aside. In another saucepan, cook onion in oil until softened. Add almonds, raisins and chili powder; stir for 3 minutes. Add rice and tomato; cook for 5 more minutes. Add broth and chicken; bring to boil. Reduce heat, cover and simmer for 15 to 20 minutes or until rice is fluffy. Makes 4 servings.

HOSTS

Richard Simmons pumps up on flavor while sweatin'-to-the-oldies

Richard Simmons, 46, is coming clean about his own eating habits. After all those antics on *Late Show with David Letterman*, after all the upbeat "Sweatin' to the Oldies" tapes, Simmons says, "I'd be lying if I said my fridge was filled with only fresh tofu and lettuce."

What he doesn't do – where most compulsive eaters in North America go wrong, he says – is "try a bunch of quick fixes and then give up. There is no magical fix for overweight people. I'm going into my 20th year of teaching people about making a commitment to a common-sense way of eating day after day after day."

So when it comes to preparing previously mundane dishes like chicken, Simmons has advice: "Give it some *flavor*!" he says. "I'm surprised there's a chicken left on the planet. There's been such a surge for chicken it's amazing. Frankly, I'm sick of chicken." Which is why Pocket Pork Chops are on his plate these days.

POCKET PORK CHOPS

2 tbsp	chicken stock	25 mL
1/4 cup	finely chopped onion	50 mL
1/4 cup	chopped mushrooms	50 mL
1/2	small apple, peeled and chopped	1/2
1 tbsp	raisins	15 mL
1/2	slice whole wheat bread, crumbled	1/2
1 tbsp	chopped parsley	15 mL
Dash	salt and pepper	Dash
1/4 tsp	Italian herbs	1 mL
2	pork loin chops (1 inch/3 cm thick)	2
1/2 cup	unsweetened applesauce	125 mL

In small skillet, heat chicken stock. Add onions, mushrooms and apple; cook until onion is softened. Meanwhile, in bowl, pour boiling water over raisins to cover; set aside for a few minutes until raisins are plumped; drain. Stir raisins, bread crumbs and seasonings into mixture in skillet. Cut a deep pocket in each pork chop. Fill with stuffing and secure with picks. In skillet coated with non-stick spray, brown chops quickly on both sides. Place chops side by side in small baking dish. Pour in enough boiling water to cover bottom of dish. Cover and bake in 350°F (180°C) oven for 35 to 45 minutes. Serve with applesauce. Makes 2 servings.

NEWS Getting the scoop on incredible edibles

Veteran anchor and world traveller **Knowlton Nash** enjoys exotic fare

Knowlton Nash, who for 10 years anchored *The National* on CBC, still remains one of the country's most familiar faces and busiest broadcasting personalities.

Currently hosting CBC's *Witness*, Nash has also written "The Microphone Wars: A History of Triumph and Betrayal at the CBC" (McClelland & Stewart, 1994), which documents behind-the-scene details at the network. With such a busy schedule, staying in shape requires a fair amount of discipline. But that doesn't mean that Nash and his wife, Lorraine Thomson, don't eat well.

Nash, who was raised on good old English-style beef and vegetables, has spent a large part of his career as a journalist outside Canada. He speaks fondly of the exotic fare he has sampled, but now he and Thomson opt for quiet dinners at home.

Seafood is a mainstay of their daily fare, and one of Nash's favorite recipes is this delicious Fillet of Sole or Grouper with Lime and Almonds.

FILLET OF SOLE OR GROUPER WITH LIME AND ALMONDS

4	sole, grouper or other fish fillet (6 oz/175 g each)	4
1/4 cup	lime juice	50 mL
3 tbsp	grated onion	45 mL
	Salt and pepper to taste	
1/3 cup	finely chopped or sliced toasted almonds	75 mL
1/4 cup	freshly grated Parmesan cheese	50 mL
	Lime slices or parsley	

Sprinkle fish with lime juice, onion, salt and pepper. Marinate in refrigerator for 1 hour. Preheat broiler. Broil fish (4 inches/10 cm below heat) for 3 minutes on one side. Turn over, sprinkle with almonds and Parmesan, and broil for another minute, until fish flakes with a fork, the cheese is melted a little and the almonds are crisp. Garnish with lime slices or parsley.

VARIATIONS:
Poached: Instead of marinating, poach the fish in 1/2 cup (125 mL) each of white wine and clam juice; drain fish, sprinkle with almonds and Parmesan, and place under broiler to melt the cheese a little.
Baked: Instead of broiling, oven-bake the marinated fish in a baking dish for about 10 minutes at 375°F (190°C); sprinkle with almonds during last 5 minutes (omit cheese).

NEWS

Dan Matheson delivers the sports, the weather and the evening meal, too

For Dan Matheson, the sports and weather anchor for *Canada AM* (CTV, weekdays), breakfast is a non-event. His days begin at 3:20 A.M, then it's "straight to work where I have my first cup of coffee of the day."

The early start would be unwelcome in most households, but it does allow Matheson to spend more time with his wife and four children, ages 9 to 14, later in the day. "I'm there when they come home and can be with them until we go to bed at 10 P.M."

The unusual hours have also meant that Matheson is responsible for most of the cooking. "I enjoy it, actually," he says. He concentrates on meals that will satisfy his children's tastes. "It's a challenge," he admits. "They'll eat pasta but not sauce, for instance; some like onions, some don't."

TERIYAKI FLANK STEAK

1-1/2 lbs	beef flank steak	750 g
1/2 cup	teriyaki sauce	125 mL
1	onion, cut in chunks	1
3	cloves garlic, minced	3
2 tbsp	honey	25 mL
	Freshly ground pepper to taste	

Slice beef into very thin strips. Combine teriyaki sauce, onion, garlic, honey and pepper. Toss with meat and allow to marinate for at least 30 minutes at room temperature or longer in refrigerator. In large skillet, stir-fry entire mixture (marinade included) briefly to desired doneness. Serve over rice. Makes 4 to 6 servings.

A self-described army brat, the Barrie, Ont. native grew up with "typical bland, British-style cooking. Everything was overdone and vegetables were reduced to paste – which my mother is semi-embarrassed by since she no longer eats like that now." Now Matheson prefers to stir-fry, sticking to a low-fat diet "more for taste than design."

Teriyaki Flank Steak (which his family calls "Sweet Beef") is a favorite. "I patterned it after a Korean dish a friend of mine makes; it's quick, easy, delicious and, best of all, all four kids love it."

NEWS

Valerie Pringle is an anchor for all seasons who likes summer best

BARBECUED BUTTERFLIED LEG OF LAMB

4 to 5 lb	boneless butterflied leg of lamb	2 to 2.5 kg
3	cloves garlic, crushed	3
1/4 cup	olive oil	50 mL
1/4 cup	lemon juice	50 mL
1/2 cup	red or white wine	125 mL
1 tbsp	Dijon mustard	15 mL
1 tbsp	honey	15 mL
1/4 cup	chopped parsley	50 mL
1/4 cup	chopped mint	50 mL

For marinade, combine garlic, oil, lemon juice, wine, mustard and honey. Place lamb in marinade and sprinkle with chopped parsley and mint. Cover and let marinate in refrigerator for 8 to 12 hours. Remove lamb, reserving marinade. Cook lamb on barbecue for 12 to 15 minutes per side or to desired doneness, brushing several times with marinade. Makes 6 to 8 servings.

Valerie Pringle knows what she likes, and in summer, it's barbecuing at her cottage in Muskoka. "I like everything about it," says the chipper co-host of *Canada AM* on CTV. "Being outside with a glass of wine, the smell of charcoal – I'll use any excuse to get one going for my family."

Her barbecue favorite is Butterflied Leg of Lamb seared over hot coals and served pink in the middle. New potatoes, vegetables and a "chockablock green salad" complete the menu. "I love shopping for food in the summer," she says, "with all the fresh vegetables and fruit."

In keeping with her philosophy of "the simpler the better," dessert on barbecue nights is always fresh fruit.

"And we prefer red wines over white," she adds, "unless of course it's a glass of sparkling cold champagne – that's the absolute *best*."

CELEBRITY COOKBOOK **31**

NEWS

Weekend anchor **Sandie Rinaldo** isn't afraid of making a mess in the kitchen

Tucked away in a desk drawer in the Toronto home of CTV *News* weekend anchor Sandie Rinaldo is a little black book filled with phone numbers her husband, Michael, would rather she forget. They're not the numbers you'd usually find. If dialed today, they'd connect you with the city's best pizza parlors, Chinese food emporiums and gourmet takeouts. "Trendy or tacky," confesses Rinaldo, "I've known and used them all."

Rinaldo, who now has three daughters, has put the world of takeout food behind her. Some time ago, she recognized that her inability to cook was a mental thing.

She transformed herself into a pretty fair cook by learning to psych herself up before entering the kitchen. "There was a time when I was first married," Rinaldo admits, "that I'd break into a cold sweat just studying a recipe."

Then a friend gave Rinaldo a copy of a quick-and-easy, 60-minute gourmet cookbook. "The book is a marvelous help to people like me – klutzes in the kitchen."

Nowadays, Rinaldo has a cooking ritual. She puts on some soothing classical music and gets out all the pots and pans she'll need so that everything is in readiness. "I know it's considered wise to clean up as you go," she says, "but I just can't do that."

Rinaldo's recipe for Chocolate-Dipped Strawberries is a favorite and meets all her requirements. Not only is it easy to prepare, but it also creates very little mess and tastes wonderful.

CHOCOLATE-DIPPED STRAWBERRIES

4 cups	fresh strawberries	1 L
6 oz	semisweet chocolate	175 g
1 tbsp	butter	15 mL
2 tsp	brandy or liqueur	10 mL

Wash strawberries but do not hull. Place on paper towels to dry. In double boiler, melt chocolate. Stir in butter and brandy. Cool slightly. Dip pointed ends of strawberries into chocolate. Place on waxed paper to set. Serve within 8 hours. Makes about 4 servings.

Wendy Mesley files a report on her kitchen career

Daily deadlines and traveling make time a precious commodity for Wendy Mesley, host of CBC's *Sunday Report*. So it's not surprising that there's little left to spend in the kitchen.

Growing up in Toronto, Mesley learned early to keep cooking simple. She picked up some basics at home but it wasn't until she started work in Montreal that she expanded her repertoire. "I did what I considered pretty fancy things at the time, like veal cutlets. I've developed a bit as a cook since then."

In recent years, her culinary skills have taken a back seat to the demands of her career. She admits her major kitchen feat has been in baking desserts. "As a matter of fact, I've learned to make pies," she says proudly. And she's learned that recipes with crumb crusts, such as her Raspberry Mousse Pie, are the most foolproof.

PHOTO: CBC

RASPBERRY MOUSSE PIE

CRUST
1-1/2 cups	graham wafer crumbs	375 mL
2 tbsp	granulated sugar	25 mL
2 tbsp	unsweetened cocoa powder	25 mL
1/4 cup	butter, melted	50 mL
1	egg white	1

FILLING
3 cups	frozen unsweetened raspberries, thawed	750 mL
1	envelope unflavored gelatin	1
1/4 cup	frozen raspberry juice concentrate, thawed	50 mL
1 cup	plain yogurt	250 mL
4	egg whites	4
1/4 cup	granulated sugar	50 mL

CRUST: Mix together crumbs, sugar, cocoa and melted butter. Whisk egg white until frothy; stir into crumbs. Press into greased 9-inch (23 cm) pie plate. Bake in 350°F (180°C) oven for 10 minutes; let cool. FILLING: In blender, purée raspberries; strain and discard seeds. In saucepan, sprinkle gelatin over juice concentrate; let stand for 1 minute, then warm over low heat until gelatin dissolves. Stir into raspberries. Chill for 30 minutes, stirring often. Stir in yogurt. Beat egg whites until they hold soft peaks; gradually add sugar, beating constantly to stiff peaks. Whisk 1/4 of egg whites into raspberry mixture, then fold in remaining whites. Pour into crust. Chill until set, about 3 hours. Makes about 8 servings.

NEWS

Alison Smith comes in from the cold to a big pot of homemade fish chowder

With nightly news duties as anchor of *The National* on Newsworld and all the travel time required for work, Alison Smith appreciates every rare weekend she can find to go skiing. She grew up in the Okanagan Valley and has been skiing since she was 10. "What I miss most about B.C. is the lakes and mountains," says Smith, who now resides in Toronto.

The independence of skiing is one of the sport's main appeals for Smith, who sees each run as a personal challenge. But even more important, it gives her valuable time with her husband and two sons.

"Skiing is one thing we do together. And it gets us out to enjoy winter instead of resenting it." Smith also associates skiing with a lot of camaraderie and good food. "We have always skied with family and friends; we always came in to a big pot of hot homemade soup."

There was a time, she says, when stews or soups were considered too unsophisticated for company. "Nowadays, people are going back to serving hearty food to guests, and they really seem to appreciate it. We serve my Fish Chowder with crusty bread, some interesting cheeses and fruit – and that's dinner."

FISH CHOWDER

1/4 cup	butter	50 mL
2 tbsp	each: finely chopped celery, onion, parsley	25 mL
1 lb	fish fillets	500 g
2 oz	each: raw shrimp, scallops, crabmeat (optional)	55 g
1	can (10 oz/284 mL) potato soup	1
2/3 cup	light cream	150 mL
2 tbsp	pernod or sherry	25 mL
Pinch	nutmeg (or to taste)	Pinch
3/4 tsp	salt	3 mL

In large heavy saucepan, melt butter. Add celery, onion and parsley; cook until softened. Add fish and cook, covered, until fish begins to flake, about 5 minutes. Stir in remaining ingredients; cook for a few minutes more and serve piping hot. Makes about 4 servings.

NEWS

Reporter **Ian Hanomansing** loves investigating diverse international cuisines

What does Vancouver-based national reporter for CBC's *Prime Time News* Ian Hanomansing make best for dinner? Reservations. And it's no joke, given the city's diversity of ethnic restaurants. The possibilities are endless, but Hanomansing usually leans toward Thai and East African spots, both of which feature versions of Coconut Chicken.

But he describes his earlier diet in university and law school as "the dark ages of fast food." During a working stint in Toronto, he bought food supplies only to make the kitchen look used when his parents visited. His father was the primary cook at home back in Sackville, N.B., but meals were mostly standard beef, chicken and potatoes – the products of the family hobby farm – despite the fact that both his schoolteacher parents came from Trinidad. It was from his aunt who cooked with a greater nod to the family's background that Hanomansing absorbed some of the Caribbean island's zesty and unique culinary tastes, if not competency in the kitchen.

Nowadays, although his office still bears empty-plate evidence of lunches on the run, he's enjoying his widened dining-out horizons and is becoming hooked on "real food."

COCONUT CHICKEN

6	chicken breasts, skinned	6
6 tbsp	butter	90 mL
2	onions, sliced	2
1	red pepper, julienned	1
3 tbsp	raisins	50 mL
1 tbsp	brown sugar	15 mL
3 tbsp	lime juice	50 mL
3/4 cup	flaked coconut	175 mL
1 tbsp	chopped fresh coriander	15 mL

In large skillet over medium heat, heat 4 tbsp (60 mL) of the butter. Brown chicken on all sides; transfer to baking dish. Add onions to skillet; cook until softened. Add red pepper, raisins, sugar and half the lime juice. Pour over chicken. Cover and bake in 375°F (190°C) oven for 10 minutes. Melt remaining butter and mix with coconut, fresh coriander and remaining lime juice. Sprinkle over chicken and bake uncovered for 10 minutes. Makes 6 servings.

NEWS

Pamela Wallin loves to spend her holiday prime time with family

For CBC's *Prime Time News* anchor Pamela Wallin, Christmas is family time, and that means an annual trip to small-town Saskatchewan. "I've spent every Christmas of my life but one in Wadena," says Wallin.

Friends and neighbors drop by without calling but, mostly, "Christmas is lots of presents and lots of food. We have Christmas Eve at my parents' house, and since the community has a lot of Ukrainian heritage, we have things like cabbage rolls and pirogis."

Christmas morning is spent opening presents at Wallin's sister's house, and everyone pitches in to make brunch – "things like pigs in blankets and homemade bread," says Wallin. She always makes the omelettes (her Turkey and Cheese Omelette is also a post-Christmas favorite for using turkey leftovers), and "then it's time to start fixing dinner back at my parents."

After a traditional turkey dinner, Wallin takes a breather and starts planning her trip home next year.

TURKEY AND CHEESE OMELETTE

2	eggs	2
2 tbsp	milk	25 mL
1/4 tsp	salt	1 mL
Dash	pepper	Dash
1 tbsp	butter	15 mL
1/2 cup	chopped cooked turkey	125 mL
1/4 cup	shredded Swiss cheese	50 mL
2 tbsp	chopped red and green pepper	25 mL

In bowl, combine eggs, milk, salt and pepper. Beat with whisk or fork until frothy. In medium-sized skillet (preferably nonstick) over medium-high heat, melt butter. Tilt pan so butter coats the inside. Pour eggs into pan and slowly tilt so eggs come partway up sides. Reduce heat and cook for about 2 minutes, until bubbles start to form on top. Add turkey, cheese and peppers. With spatula, ease eggs away from sides of pan. Lift one-third of omelette with spatula and fold toward middle. Repeat with other side. Let cook another 2 minutes. Slide omelette out of pan on to plate. Makes 1 or 2 servings.

CELEBRITY COOKBOOK

DRAMA Star grazing on heavenly fare off the air

Angela Lansbury's positive power comes from the book, she wrote

The eating plan that's made a big difference in Angela Lansbury's life isn't a diet, she says in her book "Positive Moves" (Delacorte Press, 1992). "It's not an impossibly restrictive way of eating," says the star of *Murder, She Wrote*. Whatever you call the plan, it's kept Lansbury in great shape for the past 10 years.

She follows a low-fat, high-fibre regimen that includes lots of fruit, vegetables and grains, and limited amounts of protein and fats. She never varies what she eats when she's working, which helps her maintain her weight and energy. "Breakfast is juice and melon," she says, "and I always have another fruit around 11." Lunch is a huge salad or sandwich full of vegetables, dressed with olive oil and lemon juice. On non-working days, she finds time to prepare low-fat, high-fibre recipes like her Power Loaf.

PHOTO: DAVID STRICK/ONYX

POWER LOAF

2 cups	boiling water	500 mL
1-1/2 cups	cracked wheat	375 mL
3 tbsp	shortening	50 mL
2 tbsp	honey	25 mL
1 tbsp	salt	15 mL
2	packets active dry yeast	2
2/3 cup	warm water	150 mL
4 cups	stone-ground wheat flour	1 L
1 cup	bran flakes	250 mL
3/4 cup	quick-cooking oats	175 mL
1/2 cup	wheat germ	125 mL

In large bowl, pour boiling water over cracked wheat and stir. Stir in shortening, honey and salt; let cool to lukewarm. Sprinkle yeast into warm water; let stand until frothy; add to wheat mixture. Gradually stir in 3 cups (750 mL) flour. Stir in bran flakes, oats and wheat germ. Mix very well and cover bowl with damp cloth. Let rise, about 1 hour, until doubled in bulk. Punch dough down. On floured surface, knead dough until smooth and elastic, blending in as much of remaining flour as needed if dough is sticky. Divide dough in half and place in 2 greased loaf pans. Cover and let rise in warm place until doubled. Bake in 350°F (180°C) oven for 45 minutes or until loaves are well browned and sound hollow when tapped. Makes 2 loaves.

DRAMA

Cynthia Dale's family motto explains why she never says diet

As steamy Olivia Novak on CBC's *Street Legal*, the raven-haired Cynthia Dale spent a lot of time wedged into her character's dress-for-sexy-success wardrobe. The poor girl practically had to starve herself, right?

"I did have to wear Olivia's clothes, so that acted like a diet for me," says Dale (who is currently filming CTV's *Taking the Falls*), "but I pretty well eat anything I want. I never really diet in a traditional sense. If I eat dessert one night, I won't the next."

A healthy appetite comes from growing up in a family whose motto is "You can never have too much pasta." With a real name like Ciurluini, Dale draws on a lifetime of watching relatives make their own noodles and sauces from scratch.

Coming from a big Toronto family (her brother and two sisters are also in show business), Dale says she loves cooking for large dinner parties. When the party's family, they take turns bringing dessert – often a Rich Rum Pie.

RICH RUM PIE

CRUST
1-3/4 cups	ground pecans	425 mL
1/2 cup	brown sugar	125 mL
3 tbsp	melted butter	50 mL

FILLING
1	envelope unflavored gelatin	1
1/4 cup	cold coffee	50 mL
1/4 cup	boiling water	50 mL
4	egg yolks	4
3/4 cup	granulated sugar	175 mL
1/4 cup	rum	50 mL
1-1/2 cups	whipping cream	375 mL

GARNISH (optional)
 Whipped cream,
 strawberries, pecans

CRUST: Mix together ground pecans, sugar and butter. Press into 9-inch (23 cm) pie plate. Bake in 375°F (190°C) oven for 6 minutes. Let cool.

FILLING: Sprinkle gelatin over coffee; let stand for 1 minute; add boiling water and stir to dissolve. Set aside to cool. Beat egg yolks; gradually add sugar and beat until thick. Add rum to coffee mixture; stir into egg yolk mixture. Chill until slightly thickened, about 5 minutes. Whip cream and fold into rum mixture. Pour into pie shell. Chill until set, 4 to 6 hours. Garnish with whipped cream, strawberries or pecans, if desired. Makes 6 to 8 servings.

DRAMA

Sara Botsford likes her food simple but always produces entertaining fare

On the TV newsroom series *E.N.G*, actress Sara Botsford played producer Ann Hildebrandt, a woman capable of burning off enough calories for six in a single workday. In the real world, though, Botsford admits it's not as easy to maintain her svelte self. Off-screen, she has an exercise regime which she fits in with raising three children and appearing off-Broadway in a new play called "The Cover of Life."

She is also disciplining herself to stay away from New York City's trendy restaurants, but when she does eat out, she keeps to the salad selections on the menu.

Botsford keeps her own cooking simple. On chilly days, she prepares warm comfort food – "mashed potatoes, tomato soup, rice pudding, stuff like that." For entertaining, she likes more exotic dishes with lots of aroma and color. She'll start with Hot Pepper Soup. "It couldn't be easier. You just throw a bunch of sautéed vegetables in the blender and top with sour cream and mint leaves. It looks like you spent hours over a hot stove. I like that kind of cooking."

HOT PEPPER SOUP

3 tbsp	vegetable oil	50 mL
6	sweet red peppers	6
2	onions, chopped	2
1	celery stalk, chopped	1
1	carrot, sliced	1
8 cups	vegetable stock	2 L
1/2 tsp	dried thyme	2 mL
2 tsp	minced garlic	10 mL
1/2 cup	Thai rice (or regular rice)	125 mL
	Salt and cayenne pepper	
1 cup	sour cream	250 mL
2 tbsp	chopped mint	25 mL

In large saucepan, heat oil. Slice one pepper into thin strips; sauté and set aside. Chop rest of peppers and sauté with onion, celery and carrots. Add stock, thyme and garlic; bring to boil. Add rice; simmer for 20 minutes. Purée soup in food processor. Add salt and pepper to taste. Pour soup into bowls; top with sour cream, mint and sautéed red pepper strips. Makes 6 to 8 servings.

 **DRAMA**

Lindsay Wagner stays clear of TV dinners and heads straight for the fresh veggies

Lindsay Wagner says she had an Uncle Sidney who actually believed he'd die if he didn't eat meat every day. And her mother also believed a steady stream of TV dinners provided a balanced diet.

Under the circumstances, Wagner could have grown up to eat like *The Simpsons*. But as a child of the '60s, she became a vegetarian. "It wasn't easy," says the former *Bionic Woman*. "It was hard to make that commitment."

Wagner, who has starred in many TV-movies (the most recent is "Bionic Breakdown"), remembers filming "The Paper Chase" in Toronto, where she began collecting recipes that "tasted good and were good for me. I've been collecting recipes ever since." Wagner has even compiled a vegetarian cookbook, "The High Road to Health" (Simon & Schuster, 1990), filled with all her favorite recipes including Tabbouleh Salad.

TABBOULEH SALAD

1 cup	bulgur	250 mL
	Water	
1/2 cup	chopped green onions	125 mL
4	tomatoes, diced	4
	Juice of 1 large lemon	
1	bunch parsley, chopped	1
1/3 cup	chopped fresh mint	75 mL
1 tsp	salt	5 mL
1/2 tsp	freshly ground pepper	2 mL
1/4 cup	olive oil	50 mL
	Romaine leaves	
	Black olives	

Soak bulgur in just enough water to cover, about 1 hour. (For chewier texture, soak for about 30 minutes; for softer texture, soak for up to 2 hours.) In salad bowl, combine onions, tomatoes, lemon juice, parsley, mint, salt, pepper and oil. Add soaked bulgur and mix well. Serve on bed of romaine. Garnish with black olives. Makes about 6 servings.

 **DRAMA**

Like all moms, **Carol Potter** believes in starting the day with a good breakfast

Carol Potter – TV mom to *Beverly Hills, 90210* teens Brenda and Brandon (Shannen Doherty, Jason Priestley) – is in the kitchen so much that it's tough to want to cook at home. "What real mother would cook like Cindy Walsh?" wonders Potter, who has a son of her own. "She's always in that kitchen surrounded by four kinds of vegetables and all kinds of other food. My mother told me she hasn't seen a TV mother cook like that since Donna Reed."

Potter grew up in New Jersey with two older brothers. "We ate fast, otherwise the food would be gone before you knew it. The menu didn't vary much – Mom was a chicken-and-rice person."

Potter moved to L.A. 10 years ago and is married now to actor Jeffrey Josephson. She likes to entertain when she has the time. "My specialty is pasta primavera." On days when she's not working, she'll whip up pancakes for breakfast. "I've always loved a good breakfast, so I came up with my own pancakes that have a special tang from buttermilk and a nice texture from rolled oats. They'll get your day off to a good start."

GOOD DAY PANCAKES

1 cup	rolled oats	250 mL
1/2 cup	cornmeal	125 mL
1/2 cup	powdered instant milk	125 mL
1/2 cup	water	125 mL
2 cups	buttermilk	500 mL
1 tbsp	honey	15 mL
1 cup	whole wheat flour	250 mL
1 tsp	baking soda	5 mL
1/2 tsp	salt	2 mL
2	eggs, beaten	2
	Shortening to grease griddle	

Combine oats, cornmeal, powdered milk, water, buttermilk and honey; let stand overnight. In the morning, beat in whole wheat flour, baking soda, salt and eggs. Heat greased griddle. For each pancake, drop 1/4 to 1/3 cup (50 to 75 mL) batter on griddle; let cook until bubbles pop, then flip over. Serve warm with butter and real maple syrup; garnish with yogurt and fresh fruit, if desired. Makes 4 servings.

DRAMA

Jim Byrnes likes his jazz hot and his food eclectic

As a former rowdyman turned family man, *Highlanders*'s Jim Byrnes has certainly expanded his cooking horizons. A few years ago, he became a partner in Cafe Django, an ambitious Vancouver restaurant that dispensed hot jazz and eclectic cuisine – like Jalapeno Corn Fritters – in healthy portions. Byrnes' own jazz combo, in fact, was one of the regular headliners.

Though unfortunately they had to close the doors, Byrnes says he still "loves eating and I have a real curiosity about food." Working in Vancouver (where he also shot *Neon Rider*) has culinary benefits. "Since the TV industry is so big here, the catering people are very competitive – which means the food on-set is terrific."

He also finds plenty of work in his home kitchen where he handles most of the cooking for his wife and two daughters. "Cooking for young children is a culinary test," he says. "That's when you learn exactly how many things you can do with pasta and cheese."

JALAPENO CORN FRITTERS

1 cup	all-purpose flour	250 mL
1 cup	cornmeal	250 mL
1 tsp	baking powder	5 mL
1/2 cup	water	125 mL
1	egg, separated	1
1/2	sweet red pepper, diced	1/2
1/2 cup	frozen corn kernels	125 mL
1	jalapeno pepper, seeded and diced	1
1/2	red onion, diced	1/2
1/4	bunch cilantro, chopped	1/4
1/2 tsp	salt	2 mL
1/2 tsp	pepper	2 mL
Dash	Worcestershire sauce	Dash
	Vegetable oil for frying	

In bowl, mix together flour, cornmeal and baking powder. Add water and egg yolk to dry mixture. Add red pepper, corn, jalapeno pepper, onion, cilantro, salt, pepper and Worcestershire sauce. Beat egg white to stiff peaks; fold into batter. In large saucepan, heat 4 inches (10 cm) oil to 375°F (190°C). Drop fritter batter from tablespoon into hot oil; cook until golden brown, about 4 to 5 minutes, turning once. Serve with salsa for dipping fritters. Makes 12.

DRAMA

From mussels to gingerbread, **Nana Visitor**'s favorite foods span the reaches of the galaxy

The spandex spacesuit and the elephant-trunk-nose prosthesis she wears for her part as Bajoran Major Kira Nerys on *Star Trek: Deep Space Nine* haven't turned Nana Visitor off costumes. In fact, Halloween is a favorite holiday, she says. "I love to dress up, the scarier the better."

But in or out of costume, Visitor's culinary tastes span the galaxies. Her favorites run the gamut from mussels in white wine and garlic broth to black bean and rice salad, but her most consuming passion is gingerbread.

"I've been eating gingerbread since I was six years old," she says. "It's the easiest recipe. I don't associate it with calories. I associate it with being really good for me because my mother always said,

OUT-OF-THIS-WORLD GINGERBREAD

1 cup	granulated sugar	250 mL
1 cup	canola oil	250 mL
1 cup	molasses	250 mL
2 tsp	baking soda	10 mL
1 cup	boiling water	250 mL
1 tsp	ginger	5 mL
1/2 tsp	cinnamon	2 mL
1/2 tsp	ground cloves	2 mL
2-1/2 cups	all-purpose flour	625 mL
2	eggs, well beaten	2

Combine ingredients in order given, dissolving baking soda in hot water. Pour into greased 13 x 9-inch (3.5 L) baking pan. Bake in 350°F (180°C) oven for 45 to 50 minutes or until tester inserted in centre comes out clean.

'It's got molasses in it, it's good for you.'"

Moving from New York to L.A. has also been good for Visitor. She grew up in a showbiz family and passed up Princeton to dance in the chorus and study acting. Now with a series and a son, Buster, Visitor doesn't spend too much time in the kitchen. But when she does, count on her to prepare her mother's gingerbread hot with whipped cream. Visitor jokes, "It's out-of-this-world."

DRAMA

William Shatner phases out fat and treks to a healthy diet

William Shatner's Captain Kirk on *Star Trek* was always ahead of his time, and so is Shatner himself when it comes to healthy eating. "For generations, the majority of Canadians and Americans learned to eat what wasn't good for them," he says. Shatner, who has been living in California for years, has remained high profile on the tube as host of *Rescue 911*. Currently, he's also involved with the new series *TekWar*.

Shatner is virtually a vegetarian. He avoids heavy sauces, an admission that would have been heresy in earlier days for Montrealers like himself. "We had great French restaurants with all the great sauces and I loved them all."

But now, at 63, Shatner feels a healthy diet is more important than ever. "A person's metabolism slows down every year and you need less food." His own kitchen specialties include baked potatoes done *his* way (brushed with olive oil, baked crispy on the outside and not too soft inside, then topped with peanut butter!). His favorite salad combination is endive, bean sprouts, carrots, watercress, cucumbers, avocado, tomatoes and grated cheese. And a longtime staple has been Banana-Nut Bread made with honey, bran and yogurt.

BANANA-NUT BREAD

2/3 cup	honey	150 mL
1/2 cup	butter	125 mL
2	eggs	2
1 tbsp	yogurt	15 mL
3	ripe bananas	3
1-1/2 tsp	baking soda	7 mL
1-3/4 cups	whole wheat flour	425 mL
1/4 cup	wheat bran	50 mL
1/4 tsp	salt	1 mL
1/3 cup	chopped nuts	75 mL

Cream together honey, butter, eggs and yogurt. Mash bananas well with fork; stir in 1/2 tsp (2 mL) baking soda and set aside. Mix together flour, bran, salt and remaining baking soda. Stir flour mixture into honey mixture. Add bananas; mix thoroughly. Stir in nuts. Pour into buttered 9 x 5-inch (2 L) loaf pan. Bake in 350°F (180°C) oven for 1 hour or until tester inserted in centre comes out clean. Remove from pan and cool on rack. Makes 1 loaf.

DRAMA

Theresa Saldana serves up healthy food in her Vancouver eatery

Running a restaurant can be a tricky business, but when Theresa Saldana – who plays wife to series lead Michael Chiklis on *The Commish* – decided to become a partner in the Vancouver eatery Carpaccio's, it was simply an extension of her own approach to eating. "Our menu happens to be very healthy, though it is not strictly vegetarian," she says. "There's also plenty for people who like their beef or chicken." Saldana, who adheres to a mostly vegetarian diet herself, has divided the Italian cuisine at the restaurant into "traditional" and "healthy."

She and her partner, head chef Mona Batal, have introduced dishes such as beef carpaccio, fresh bocconcini and tomato salad, fusilli with seafood and curry cream, penne chicken chorizo, tiramisu and – Saldana's favorite – the vegetarian Theresa Pizza. "I started making it at home on pita breads because it was quick and easy," she says, "but Mona added the big chunks of garlic to make it even yummier."

The decor at Carpaccio's is as eclectic as the menu, combining Batal's collection of Mexican masks with autographed photos of stars who've wined and dined there, including Billy Joel, Kirstie Alley, Perry King and Olympia Dukakis. "I feel good about bringing people to a warm atmosphere," says Saldana, "whether I'm inviting people from the show as my guests or just directing people who are new in Vancouver to a good meal."

THERESA PIZZA

4 oz	spinach, blanched	125 g
3 oz	diced, grilled eggplant	90 g
4	roasted garlic cloves	4
3 oz	feta cheese	90 g
1 oz	julienned zucchini	30 g
2 oz	tomato sauce	60 mL
4 oz	mozzarella cheese	125 g

Using your favorite pizza dough or an unsplit whole wheat pita, arrange ingredients on crust and bake in 350°F (180°C) oven for approximately 30 minutes. Serves 1.

 **DRAMA**

Kathy Baker has an Emmy and a diploma from the Paris Cordon Bleu

Ladies and gentlemen, an Emmy-winning actress who has a coveted Le Grande Diplome from the renowned Paris Cordon Bleu! "It was kind of accidental," says Kathy Baker, who plays Dr. Jill Brock on *Picket Fences*.

Her mother, who was born and raised in Paris, loved to cook all the while Baker grew up in Albuquerque, N.M., and San Francisco. "She taught me to love cooking, too," says Baker. "Then when I got my degree in French from Berkeley, I wanted to go to France to actually speak the language for a while."

Baker explains: "My godfather in Paris – who had always wanted to study at Le Cordon Bleu – suggested I apply, and I wound up practising the language as a chef in a restaurant."

APPLE CRISP

6 to 9	crisp tasty apples	6 to 9
1/2 cup	butter or margarine	125 mL
1 cup	all-purpose flour	250 mL
1 cup	granulated sugar	250 mL
	Cinnamon	

Peel, core and slice apples. Place them in bowl of cold water. Combine butter, flour and sugar; blend together until crumbly. Drain apples and add sprinkle of cinnamon. Arrange apples in 9-inch (2.5 L) square pan; cover with flour mixture. Bake in 350°F (180°C) oven for 30 minutes or until apples are tender. Makes about 4 servings.

Back in the U.S., Baker supported herself with occasional cooking jobs during the early years of stage work. Now living in Los Angeles with her husband and two young sons, she says she uses her cordon bleu training primarily "to tell at a glance whether a recipe is any good."

She also knows the value of keeping things simple, especially now that *Picket Fences* has been on the air for three seasons. "I've just got a regular old kitchen," she says. "You don't need a lot of fancy equipment to cook well." And you don't need fancy recipes either. The family favorite is a simple Apple Crisp. "I've never made it that someone didn't rave about it, and it's great comfort food, too."

DRAMA

Nora Ephron's Tiramisu is the dating dessert of the '90s

"What is tiramisu?"
"You'll find out."
"What is it?"
"Some woman is going to want me to do it to her, and I'm not going to know what it is."
"You'll love it."
"This is going to be much tougher than I thought it would be."

– *Widower Sam Baldwin (Tom Hanks) and friend Jay (Rob Reiner) discuss dating in the '90s in "Sleepless in Seattle."*

In honor of the Oscars, we've come up with our own category: Funniest Food-Related Scene in a Full-Length Feature. And the winner is ..."Sleepless in Seattle," which drew a Best Original Screenplay nomination for writer-director Nora Ephron (who, naturally, is also a gourmet cook and provides her own Tiramisu recipe) and also a nomination for Best Original Song.

Food has often been prominent in the movies. *Entertainment Tonight's* Leonard Maltin says: "The ultimate food films have to be 'Babette's Feast' and 'Like Water for Chocolate.' The connection between food and sensuality has been done before, but seldom as well."

TIRAMISU

1	package of soft ladyfingers (about 22)	1
4	fresh eggs	4
1/2 cup	coffee liqueur or brandy	125 mL
1 lb	mascarpone cheese	500 g
1/2 cup	granulated sugar	125 mL
1/2 cup	strong espresso	125 mL
2 oz	semisweet chocolate, grated	60 g

Allow ladyfingers to dry out slightly. Separate eggs into 2 large bowls. Add liqueur to yolks; beat until blended. Add mascarpone; beat until blended. Beat egg whites until they hold soft peaks; continue to beat, adding sugar a little at a time, until stiff peaks are formed. Stir half the egg whites into cheese mixture, then fold in remaining whites. Set aside. Dip ladyfingers in espresso; don't saturate. Place half of ladyfingers, flat side down, in shallow dish. Cover with half the cheese mixture; smooth the top. Grate half the chocolate over top. Add another layer of espresso-dipped ladyfingers. Cover with remaining cheese mixture and smooth the top. Cover with remaining chocolate. Refrigerate, covered, for several hours. Can also be assembled in individual dishes. Makes about 12 servings.

PHOTO: BRUCE MCBROOM/TRI-STAR PICTURES

DRAMA

Sweet-16 **Sarah Polley** embraces Christmas traditions past and present

Although she plays a character (Sara Stanley) from the early 1900s, Sarah Polley of CBC's *Road to Avonlea* is planted in today's real world, especially at Christmas.

"I try to donate time to the food bank, and I think it's cool when friends give a donation to charity in my name as a Christmas present," says the 16-year-old Polley.

Christmas morning finds Polley and her family – father, brothers, sisters, aunts and cousins – around the tree in Toronto, opening presents. And Christmas dinner is really special. "Dad's an amazing cook and we'll probably have roast goose in Grand Marnier sauce with all the trimmings. And because Dad's British, we'll have a flaming Christmas pudding."

Polley says that in Sara Stanley's day Christmas tradition would call for skating or tobogganing, and books and homemade crafts as presents. "They'd probably have oranges for a treat because they were rare back then, especially in winter. Their dinner would probably be turkey, with a flaming pudding just like ours."

MARILLA'S PLUM PUDDING

1 cup	all-purpose flour	250 mL
1/2 cup	granulated sugar	125 mL
1/2 cup	fresh bread crumbs	125 mL
1/2 tsp	each: baking powder, salt, cinnamon, nutmeg	2 mL
1/2 cup	butter	125 mL
1/2 cup	each: chopped raisins and currants	125 mL
1/4 cup	chopped walnuts	50 mL
1	egg, beaten	1
1/2 cup	hot milk	125 mL
1/4 cup	molasses	50 mL

Grease 4-cup (1 L) pudding mold and sprinkle with granulated sugar. In large bowl, mix together flour, sugar, bread crumbs, baking powder, salt, cinnamon and nutmeg. Cut in butter until mixture forms coarse crumbs. Toss raisins and currants with a little flour and add, with walnuts, to mixture. Add egg, milk and molasses; mix well. Spoon into mold. Cover with double layer of foil (grease the side next to the pudding); tie foil with string. Set mold on rack in large pot of boiling water halfway up sides of mold. Cover and steam, about 3 hours or until toothpick inserted in pudding comes out clean. Set on cooling rack, remove foil and let stand for 10 minutes. Invert onto warmed serving dish. Serve with your favorite sauce. Makes about 8 servings.

DRAMA

For **Tom Jackson**, bread is the staff of life north of 60

"It's usually a *real* special occasion if I do the cooking," laughs Tom Jackson, who plays Band Chief Peter Kenidi on CBC's *North of 60*. "My wife and I eat out a lot, but being on the road for 30 years makes restaurant food as much being home as being home."

Jackson makes his home today in Winnipeg, but home cooking brings back memories of his childhood on the One Arrow Reserve near Saskatoon. He's in tune with city food, but recently at a charity golf tournament, "a woman was serving Bannock and Saskatoon Berry Soup, and I made sure I got her recipes. Bannock is a way of life in northern communities, a bread served at almost every meal," he explains. "It tastes fabulous and is the ultimate comfort food."

When not working or golfing, Jackson is raising money to feed the homeless. "I see the entertainment business as a means to an end," he says, "the end being the charity work that I do."

BANNOCK

2 cups	all-purpose flour	500 mL
1 tbsp	baking powder	15 mL
2 tsp	granulated sugar	10 mL
1 tsp	salt	5 mL
1/4 cup	lard	50 mL
3/4 cup	(approx.) water	175 mL

In bowl, mix together flour, baking powder, sugar and salt. Cut in lard. Stir in enough water to make a soft, slightly sticky dough. Form into ball and knead lightly on floured surface until smooth. On greased and floured baking sheet, pat or roll dough to about 1-1/2 inch (4 cm) thickness. Bake in 400°F (200°C) oven for about 30 minutes or until browned and baked through.

SASKATOON BERRY SOUP

2 cups	saskatoon berries (or blueberries)	500 mL
2 cups	water	500 mL
1/3 cup	sugar (or to taste)	75 mL
Dash	cinnamon	Dash
1 tbsp	cornstarch	15 mL
1 tbsp	cold water	15 mL

In saucepan, combine berries and water; bring to boil; simmer for 10 minutes. Stir in sugar and cinnamon. Mix cornstarch and water; stir into soup; cook until thickened. Makes 4 servings.

DRAMA

Food lover **Michael Tucker's** favorite law is double-sauce it

It's no accident that the writers of L.A. Law portrayed Stuart Markowitz as an appreciator of fine food. In real life, that's just the way Michael Tucker is. "In one of my favorite episodes," he says, "I was on the outs with Ann (Jill Eikenberry, his series and real-life wife). I showered her with delicacies, and finally she came around." Pause, laughter. "I can't say that it hasn't worked that way once in a while in our marriage."

Tucker says, "I learned Italian cooking while I was doing a movie in Rome. If God created veal piccata, I think it's up to me and Jill to eat it, for crying out loud."

Eikenberry is more conservative about calories, but Tucker's basic rule of thumb when it comes to pasta is "double-sauce it." He explains: "Sauce it when you drain it and sauce it *again* when you eat it. Also, as a ground rule, add more cheese than you think is necessary."

Now that the series has ended, Tucker and Eikenberry have time to enjoy picnics together although Tucker is working on a book due out in the fall of '95. Along with a bottle of chilled wine, the picnic basket is sure to feature Tucker's special Peasant Picnic Loaf.

PEASANT PICNIC LOAF

1	round Italian loaf (8-inch/20 cm diameter)	1
1/2 lb	sliced salami	250 g
1/4 lb	sliced prosciutto	125 g
12	large black olives, halved	12
4	artichoke hearts, halved	4
6 oz	mozzarella cheese, sliced	175 g
4	sun-dried tomatoes, halved	4
2	tomatoes, sliced	2
1/4 cup	olive oil	50 mL
	Salt and pepper	

Slice off top of bread and set aside. Scoop out most of inside of loaf, leaving 1-inch (3 cm) shell. Layer remaining ingredients in shell and drizzle oil over top. Sprinkle with salt and pepper to taste. Replace top of loaf and wrap with foil. Refrigerate overnight. Cut in wedges. Makes 6 to 8 servings.

 **DRAMA**

Ex-football player **Carl Weathers** doesn't pass on a fully stocked kitchen

Eating used to simply be a way of feeding my body," says Carl Weathers, "but now I try to bring a little artistry to it." Starring as the police chief in *In the Heat of the Night*, the football-player-turned-actor has a very well-equipped kitchen in his Los Angeles home and made a point of similarly equipping his rented suburban townhouse near Atlanta, where the series was filmed.

Weathers also spruced up his kitchen when he was in Vancouver shooting *Street Justice*. "Anywhere I'm based for a while, I spend a lot of money on cookware. If I combined all the stuff I've bought over the years, I could start a restaurant."

Weathers, who shares custody of his two sons, says, "I always cook for them when they're at my house in Los Angeles. I do fried chicken with my own 27 herbs and spices." He swears, "people who've had my chicken will testify they've never had better."

SOUR CREAM CUCUMBER DIP

2	large cucumbers	2
4 cups	sour cream	1 L
1/2 cup	chopped fresh herbs (chives, mint, parsley, tarragon or combination)	125 mL
	Salt and pepper to taste	

Peel, seed and grate cucumbers; place in strainer and squeeze out excess liquid. Mix cucumber with sour cream, herbs, salt and pepper. Refrigerate until ready to serve. For presentation, cut tops off a red, yellow and green pepper; scoop out the insides. Ladle dip into pepper shells. Place in middle of platter of fresh mixed vegetables for dipping.

A former Oakland Raider from 1970 to '71 – "The Raiders were a beer-mentality team then, always brawling but always winning" – and, later, a B.C. Lion, Weathers follows pro football whenever he can, especially big events like the playoffs and the Super Bowl.

"I enjoy having people over for game parties," he says. "My fried chicken always goes over great at that kind of gathering. And for just nibbling, I always fix my Sour Cream Cucumber Dip with fresh vegetables. It's one of those things that can be greatly enhanced by presentation, too. I scoop out different colored peppers and put the dip in those."

DRAMA

Actor **Chris Potter** eats all day to keep himself fighting and animated

Cooking is one thing that busy actor Chris Potter generally puts on the back burner. "I'm working 12-hour days," says the London, Ont. native who juggles roles as action heroes on two hit shows. Potter's best known for playing Peter, crime-fighting son of Caine (David Carradine) on Kung Fu: The Legend Continues, but he is also the voice of Gambit on the popular animated TV series X-Men.

"I eat all day," says Potter. His diet tends to be low fat with an international flavor. "I'm in Toronto's Chinatown all the time shooting Kung Fu, so I eat a lot of Chinese food." When time allows, Potter enjoys cooking up a batch of minestrone. "My mom started making the soup, and now I make a big pot to last the weekend. It's quick, filling and nutritious."

MINESTRONE SOUP

1-1/2 lbs	lean ground beef	750 g
1	onion, chopped	1
1	celery stalk, chopped	1
1	can (28 oz/796 mL) tomatoes	1
2	cans (10 oz/284 mL) onion soup	2
5 cups	water	1.25 L
1	small package frozen mixed vegetables	1
1	jar (375 mL) spaghetti sauce	1
1/2 cup	small pasta	125 mL
2 tbsp	chopped parsley	25 mL
1-1/2 tsp	granulated sugar	7 mL
1/2 tsp	each: thyme, oregano, basil (or to taste)	2 mL

Salt and pepper to taste
Grated Parmesan cheese

In large saucepan, brown ground beef lightly. Add onion and celery; cook until softened. Add tomatoes, onion soup and water. Bring to boil. Add vegetables cover and simmer for 30 minutes. Add spaghetti sauce, pasta, parsley, sugar, herbs, salt and pepper (if needed). Simmer uncovered for 30 minutes, stirring occasionally. Sprinkle each serving with grated Parmesan and serve with Italian bread. Makes about 8 servings.

COMEDY Funny folk get serious about their food

The talk's nothing but the food's something at **Seinfeld**'s local diner

LAMB SHISH KEBABS

1/2 cup	olive oil	125 mL
	Juice of 1 lemon	
2	cloves garlic, minced	2
1 tsp	oregano	5 mL
	Salt and pepper to taste	
1-1/4 lbs	boneless lamb, cubed	625 g
	Cherry tomatoes	
	Sweet pepper wedges	
	Onion wedges	

In bowl, combine olive oil, lemon juice, garlic, oregano, salt and pepper. Add meat and marinate in refrigerator for 24 to 48 hours. Alternate meat and vegetables on skewers. Broil for 10 to 15 minutes, turning halfway through cooking. Serve over steamed rice with green peas. Makes 4 servings.

Seen from the outside only as Restaurant, the diner on *Seinfeld* is actually known to generations of New Yorkers as Tom's Restaurant, and it's been at 2880 Broadway on the Upper West Side since the '30s.

"I guess we should really put up a picture of Jerry Seinfeld," says manager Michael Zoulis, whose family has been in charge of Tom's through most of its history. Seinfeld had in fact eaten at Tom's before it ever became linked with the hit comedy, but an executive producer actually picked the exterior shot over several other contenders. Inside, Tom's looks less like a coffee shop than the Hollywood set used on *Seinfeld* does.

And although the menu includes food as American as hamburgers, most of the personnel have roots in the Greek island of Kasos. Part of the charm of Tom's is hearing the waitresses yelling food orders in Greek, and the call often goes out for the house specialty – Lamb Shish Kebabs.

PHOTO: THE EVERETT COLLECTION INC.

COMEDY

No more growing pains for Alan Thicke – life's too sweet

Alan Thicke's rambling ranch house north of Los Angeles has a full-time cook, and elaborate gatherings are catered.

But Thicke still makes it into the big kitchen occasionally to fix his favorite recipes, such as duck with peach sauce. "I have a sweet tooth," he says, "and I love duck, so to make duck taste like dessert is very appealing." As for real desserts, Key Lime Pie is a favorite.

Thicke, a native of Kirkland Lake, Ont., also says his cooking has improved a lot since his student days at the University of Western Ontario. The one dish he made for his roommates was "$5 casserole – hamburger, potatoes, corn and ketchup woven together."

Thicke began his career writing comedy for CBC. He moved to Hollywood in the '70s and starred in the hit sitcom *Growing Pains* from 1985 to '92. Since then, other projects have kept him on the move, but Thicke, recently married to former Miss World Gina Marie Tolleson and close to two sons from his marriage to Gloria Loring, says he's settled down and life is sweet (especially when Key Lime Pie is on the menu).

KEY LIME PIE

CRUST

1-1/4 cups	graham wafer crumbs	300 mL
1 tsp	granulated sugar	5 mL
1/3 cup	melted butter	75 mL

FILLING

3	egg yolks	3
1	can (300 mL) condensed milk	1
3/4 cup	fresh lime juice	175 mL

MERINGUE

3	egg whites	3
1/4 tsp	cream of tartar	1 mL
6 tbsp	granulated sugar	90 mL

CRUST: Combine ingredients and mix well. Press into 9-inch (23 cm) pie plate. Bake in 375°F (190°C) oven for 8 minutes. FILLING: Beat egg yolks until thick; beat in condensed milk. Add lime juice slowly. If desired, blend in few drops of green food coloring to give soft green color. Pour into crust. Bake in 350°F (180°C) oven for 10 minutes. MERINGUE: Beat egg whites with cream of tartar until they hold soft peaks. Gradually add sugar, beating constantly to stiff peaks. Spread over pie to edges. Bake in 350°F (180°C) oven for 10 minutes or until very lightly browned. Cool thoroughly. Makes about 6 servings.

COMEDY

The way to **Homer Simpson's** heart is through his stomach

Mmmmmmmmmmm, pork chops! Yeah, no doubt about it, pork chops are definitely at the top of Homer Simpson's all-time favorite food list. Just ask some of the actors who provide voices on *The Simpsons*, or some of the writers on the show, and they all agree – even pickled eggs, beef jerky, donuts, chocolate and beer don't do it for Homer like pork chops.

One of those especially familiar with Homer's eating habits is Hank Azaria. Besides supplying the voices of bartender Moe, Kwik-E-Mart owner Apu, police chief Wiggum, he also played Nick Riviera, MD, the Ricky Ricardo-voiced doctor who performed heart-bypass surgery on Homer.

"I think Dr. Nick would say that the only thing bigger than Homer's heart is his stomach," says Azaria. "Once Homer was on his way to throwing out a spoiled submarine sandwich but he couldn't resist finishing it off. He got sick, but he was true to his stomach."

As Moe, Azaria has seen Homer down many a pickled egg at the bar – including the ones Homer once washed down "by chug-a-lugging the pickle brine." But, although Homer is known to try almost anything, not even *he* would eat Marge's "three-eyed" fish the night his boss, Mr. Burns, came to dinner.

At the Kwik-E-Mart, Homer's hit-and-run special is beef jerky. Donuts qualify anywhere, anytime. And despite Homer's heart scare and half-hearted diet attempts, wife Marge seems resigned to the fact that a man has to eat what he has to eat – her easy-to-fix *Simpson*'s style Breaded Pork Chops.

BREADED PORK CHOPS		
4	pork chops	4
1	egg	1
1 tbsp	water	15 mL
1 cup	fine breadcrumbs	250 mL
	Salt and pepper	
3 tbsp	vegetable oil	50 mL

In dish, beat egg with water. Put breadcrumbs in another dish. Dip each chop into egg, then into breadcrumbs to coat evenly. Sprinkle on both sides with salt and pepper. Let stand 15 minutes. In skillet over medium heat, heat oil. Fry chops for 3 to 4 minutes per side or until golden brown and just until cooked through. Makes 2 to 4 servings.

COMEDY

Comedian **Cheech Marin** is king of the palace kitchen

Long before he landed the role of chef Chuy Castillos on *The Golden Palace*, and even before his wild and crazy Cheech & Chong days, Cheech Marin worked as a chef – in Banff, Alta. "I went there to become a ski bum," says Marin, "and ended up working in the kitchen of a resort. I worked under some really good chefs who taught me a lot about cooking, and I learned to ski at the same time."

Now the father of three has become king of his own kitchen. "I cook everyday, especially on the barbecue." And true to his heritage, the east L.A. native prefers Mexican-American food. "I just did Beef Machaca the other night."

Food even plays a part in one of Marin's upcoming projects. "I'm doing a film about a guy whose face appears on a tortilla, setting off a whole train of events!" And if things don't work out with his career, Marin jokes that he can always slalom back into the kitchen.

BEEF MACHACA

1 lb	flank steak	500 g
1-1/2 tsp	oregano	7 mL
	Salt and pepper	
1	medium onion, chopped	1
1 tbsp	vegetable oil	15 mL
1	can (28 oz/796 mL) tomatoes	1
1	can (about 4 oz/125 mL) mild chilies, chopped	1
1	large potato, peeled and cubed	1
1	can (10 oz/284 mL) chicken broth	1
	Tortillas	

Pound steak well until thin. Season with half the oregano, and salt and pepper to taste. Broil, turning once, until well done. Meanwhile, in saucepan, cook onion in oil until softened. Add tomatoes (chopped or crushed) and their juice. Add chilies and remaining oregano; bring to boil. Add potato; reduce heat and simmer for about 30 minutes. Meanwhile, pound steak again and separate into threads or chop finely. Add meat to sauce; stir in chicken broth. Simmer for 1-1/2 hours, adding liquid (water or more stock) as needed. Spoon mixture onto tortillas and roll up. Makes 4 servings.

COMEDY

Red Green may sauté hamster but **Steve Smith** leaves the cooking to his wife

When the dinner bell rings at Possum Lodge, located just over the edge of the Canadian wilderness, Red Green is probably serving up some time-honored backwoods disaster, such as his specialty – sautéed hamster. "The best thing about it," says Red, "is that most of the ingredients can be found within a 50-foot radius of your chair." That includes a capful of battery acid and a gallon of 10W40 motor oil.

The *New Red Green Show* is the brainchild of its star, Steve Smith, who turned a hardly original idea – men are idiots – into a North American cult phenomenon.

Smith admits that Morag, his wife (and partner on an earlier series) is the family chef. "We have a traditional relationship," he says. "Whatever we serve, people always ask *her* for the recipe."

GRILLED PORK TENDERLOIN

	Wooden skewers (8 in/20 cm)	
1-1/2 lbs	pork tenderloin	750 g
1/4 cup	butter	50 mL
1 tbsp	lemon juice	15 mL
	Grated lemon rind	
1/2 tsp	Tabasco sauce	2 mL
3 tbsp	grated onion	50 mL
3 tbsp	brown sugar	50 mL
1 tsp	ground coriander	5 mL
1/2 tsp	ground cumin	2 mL
1/4 tsp	ground ginger	1 mL
1	clove garlic, crushed	1
1/2 cup	Indonesian soy sauce or teriyaki sauce	125 mL
	Salt and pepper to taste	

Soak wooden skewers in water for 30 minutes so they don't scorch. Cut pork into 1-inch (3 cm) cubes; place in shallow dish. In saucepan, melt butter and add remaining ingredients. Bring to boil and simmer for 5 minutes. Pour over meat; let marinate for about 30 minutes. (Butter may congeal, but don't worry.) Remove meat, reserving marinade, and put 5 or 6 pieces on each skewer. Grill on barbecue for 15 minutes or just until cooked through (don't overcook), turning frequently. Remove meat from skewers to a platter. Reheat marinade to boiling; pour over meat. Serve on a bed of rice. Great with spinach salad. Makes 6 to 8 servings.

COMEDY

Something special in the food gives it a **Northern Exposure**

There must be something in the clean mountain air of Cicely, Alaska – home of the quirky citizens of *Northern Exposure* – that inspires good eating. And since many of the show's references are actually framed around food – such as Dr. Joel Fleischman's constant craving for New York deli sandwiches, Maurice's esoteric gourmet feasts or the burgers 'n' beer fare served at The Brick – it was only natural that the popular series would inspire "The Northern Exposure Cookbook" (Contemporary Books, 1993).

Where it became tricky, though, was getting the recipes from some of the more unusual locals – particularly the town's resident recluse and gourmet chef, Adam, who was temperamental about sharing his recipes.

That aside, the whole town agrees that his recipe for Cumin Noodles (inspired by the 1990 episode "Aurora Borealis") is a gourmet work of art. Adam's last name is a mystery but, even Maurice admits, "his cumin noodles will make you shut your eyes with pleasure."

CUMIN NOODLES

1/2 lb	fresh Chinese noodles (or linguine)	250 g
2 tbsp	vegetable oil	25 mL
1/2 lb	boneless chicken breast, thinly sliced	250 g
1 tbsp	soy sauce	15 mL
1 tbsp	sesame oil (or to taste)	15 mL
2 tsp	ground cumin	10 mL
1/2 cup	chicken stock	125 mL
2	green onions, cut in 1-inch (3 cm) pieces	2

Fill 12-cup (3 L) saucepan halfway with water and bring to boil. Add noodles, bring back to boil, reduce heat to medium and cook for 5 minutes. Drain noodles and rinse with water. Heat vegetable oil in wok over medium heat. Add chicken and cook for 2 minutes, stirring constantly. Add noodles and stir in soy sauce, sesame oil, cumin, chicken stock and onions. Raise heat and cook for another 2 minutes, stirring constantly. Makes 4 to 6 servings.

COMEDY

Tom Bosley is a familiar face on stage, screen, TV and in the kitchen, too

Tom Bosley, who played Father Dowling and Amos Tupper (the original sheriff on *Murder, She Wrote*) and now Belle's father in the Broadway musical version of "Beauty and the Beast," has long been a familiar face. But with hundreds of stage, screen and TV appearances to his credit, it is his 11-year stint as Richie's dad on *Happy Days* for which he will be remembered best.

When his busy schedule limits him to just two meals a day, everyone's favorite dad does his best to enjoy those meals.

"My grandmother lived with us for many years," Bosley recalls, "and she was a wonderful cook. She was German and made things like noodle kugels, brisket of beef, potato pancakes and great chopped liver." But while the Chicago native has been an avowed meat lover all his life, his eating habits have had to adjust to the very different tastes of his family now. His wife and two of his daughters are almost total vegetarians.

Although his cooking skills are limited, he does have specialties such as "the best scrambled eggs of anybody" and a meatless Linguine with Red Clam Sauce that satisfies his cravings for hearty food.

LINGUINE WITH RED CLAM SAUCE

2 tbsp	olive oil	25 mL
1	clove garlic, minced	1
1/4 cup	chopped onion	50 mL
2-1/2 cups	crushed tomatoes with juice	625 mL
1/2 tsp	dried oregano	2 mL
1/4 tsp	dried basil	1 mL
2 tbsp	chopped fresh parsley	25 mL
1 cup	canned baby clams, drained and minced	250 mL
1 lb	linguine	500 g
1/4 cup	freshly grated Parmesan cheese	50 mL

In heavy skillet or pot, heat oil. Add garlic and onion; cook until softened. Add tomatoes, oregano, basil, parsley, and salt and pepper to taste. Simmer for 15 minutes, stirring occasionally. Add clams and simmer another 5 minutes. Meanwhile, in large pot of boiling salted water, cook linguine until tender but firm; drain. Spoon sauce on top and sprinkle with Parmesan. Serves 4.

COMEDY

When **Roseanne** cooks at home, something's always stewing

One thing *Roseanne* is not known for is her culinary expertise – the height of her cooking on the hit weekly series seems to be ordering pizza. In real life, the Emmy Award-winning actress-comedienne has redefined her eating habits and, along the way, dropped 70 pounds.

Roseanne's interest in food also led her to a new career in 1993. It seems that life imitates art: After opening a lunch counter on the show, Roseanne launched her own restaurant (with then-husband Tom Arnold) – Roseanne and Tom's Big Food Diner – in Eldon, Iowa. The menu is "real diner food, although we also serve turkey burgers. That's as California as it gets," jokes Roseanne.

When Roseanne cooks at home, the meals are healthy and low fat. "I make turkey meatloaf and tuna fish casseroles. Despite all this money I have, those are my two favorite meals." Another favorite of Roseanne's is a great seafood stew, Cioppino.

PHOTO: GEORGE LANGE/ONYX

CIOPPINO

1 tsp	olive oil	5 mL
1 cup	chopped onions	250 mL
1 cup	chopped green peppers	250 mL
1/2 cup	chopped celery	125 mL
1/4 cup	chopped green onions	50 mL
1-1/2 tsp	chopped garlic	7 mL
1	can (48 oz/1.36 L) mixed vegetable or tomato juice	1
1	can (28 oz/796 mL) whole tomatoes	1
1	vegetable bouillon cube	1
1	bay leaf	1
1-1/2 tsp	red pepper sauce	7 mL
1/2 tsp	Cajun fish seasoning	2 mL
12	each: clams and mussels, scrubbed	12
1/2 lb	each: medium shrimp (peeled and deveined), sea bass fillets and crab legs	250 g

In Dutch oven, heat oil over medium-high heat. Add chopped vegetables and garlic. Cook, stirring occasionally, until tender, about 10 minutes. Stir in juice, tomatoes, bouillon cube, bay leaf, red pepper sauce and Cajun fish seasoning. Bring to boil; reduce heat and simmer uncovered for 1 hour. Cut sea bass filets and crab legs into 1-inch (3 cm) pieces. Stir in seafood, cover and cook until clam and mussel shells are opened, about 5 to 8 minutes. Discard any unopened shells and bay leaf. Makes about 4 servings.

 **COMEDY**

Judith Light takes the cake when she wants 'cause she knows who's the boss

Judith Light never dreamed she would make her living offering up laughs as one of TV's most popular moms, Angela Bower on *Who's the Boss?* "I went through a very difficult time," she says, referring to a weight problem that took a lot of hard work to change. Today, she's slim, fit and the picture of health. But that great figure didn't just happen all by itself. She avoids junk food, does 100 sit-ups daily, combines exercise with lots of good nutrition – and would give it all up in a minute if she could.

But having looked at pounds from both sides now, Light, a two-time Emmy winner for *One Life to Live*, says she's hooked on being and looking healthy.

"I don't want to make platitudes for anybody. You have to find out what works best for your lifestyle. And I don't believe in denial. If I want chocolate cake, I'll cut a small piece. I just won't eat the whole cake."

So now who's the boss? Judith Light is – at least when it comes to the battle of the bulge.

LIGHT MUSTARD CHICKEN

4	skinless, boneless chicken breasts	4
1 tbsp	olive oil	5 mL
2	cloves garlic, minced	2
3 tbsp	white wine	50 mL
3 tbsp	low-sodium soy sauce	50 mL
2 tbsp	Moutarde de Meaux or other strong-flavored mustard	25 mL
2 tbsp	capers	25 mL

Cut chicken into 1/2-inch (1 cm) strips or 1-inch (3 cm) cubes. In skillet, heat oil. Add garlic and cook until lightly golden. Add chicken and cook, stirring, until slightly brown. Add wine and soy sauce; cook, stirring, for 2 minutes. Add mustard and capers. Continue stirring until chicken is just cooked through (2 to 3 minutes). Makes 4 servings.

COMEDY

Wonderful TV mom **Alley Mills** dips into the '60s but woks in the '90s

LOBSTER DIP

2 cups	sour cream	500 mL
1/4 cup	mayonnaise	50 mL
1 tbsp	lemon juice	15 mL
1/4 tsp	salt	1 mL
1 tsp	dried dillweed	5 mL
1 tsp	dried green onions (or 1 tbsp/15 mL chopped fresh)	5 mL
2 cups	flaked lobster meat	500 mL

Combine all ingredients and chill for about 1 hour. Serve with crackers or fresh vegetables for dipping. Makes 6 to 8 servings.

As Norma Arnold, suburban housewife from the '60s on *The Wonder Years*, Alley Mills was constantly cooking. "It seemed as if every shot I was in had me at the stove," says Mills. "But the joke with the cast and crew was that Norma never made anything but chili. I was always reaching for something from the shelf – cinnamon or paprika – but the dish I was making always looked like chili."

At home in Los Angeles and married to *Dr. Quinn, Medicine Woman*'s Orson Bean (Loren Bray), Mills is Norma-like in one respect. "When friends come for dinner, I really care how the table looks. Fresh flowers matter a lot. And I don't have matching plates, but they're all from antique stores and kind of mix and match together."

Even though she grew up in New York, Mills' primary diet was Southern-fried cooking. "My mother always worked and a Southern woman cooked for us – fried chicken, cornbread and apple fritters." Now Mills relies heavily on wok cooking. "I stir-fry all kinds of stuff – broccoli, scallions, mushrooms, zucchini – with garlic, ginger and sesame oil."

Alley Mills' Lobster Dip evokes memories of party time in the '60s but is still a crowd pleaser in the '90s.

COMEDY

Bob Newhart used to like chipped beef, but now he's big on barbecue

Bob Newhart is a travelin' man. When he's not taping a series or on the golf course or performing in concert (which he's been doing for the past 35 years), he's likely to be toting his family around the globe, partaking of some pretty fancy cuisine. But like the down-to-earth innkeeper he played on *Newhart*, the actor's tastes remain simple. "I'd like to see peanut butter served in the finer restaurants everywhere: creamy on wholewheat bread with strawberry jelly."

While also admitting to being "the only guy in the barracks who liked chipped beef on toast" during his stint in the army years ago, he credits family trips (with wife Ginney and their four children) to Europe for doing wonders for his pedestrian palate. Trips to Italy, especially, have transformed Newhart's tastes, and he's a big fan of Italian cooking. Dining abroad, he also learned to "like things that I wouldn't have tried otherwise, like swordfish and liver."

Back home in Bel Air, family cookouts (with Ginney manning the barbecue) are regular events and you'll often find Bob's Barbecue Chicken on the grill.

BARBECUE CHICKEN

4	chicken breasts (bone-in)	4
3/4 cup	tomato sauce	175 mL
1/2 cup	beef broth	125 mL
2 tbsp	tomato paste	25 mL
1 tbsp	red wine vinegar	15 mL
2 tsp	liquid smoke	10 mL
1 tbsp	brown sugar	15 mL
1 tbsp	garlic pepper, finely crushed	15 mL
1 tsp	garlic powder	5 mL
1 tsp	onion powder	5 mL
1 tsp	paprika	5 mL
	Cayenne pepper to taste	

Place chicken in microwavable baking dish. Mix together remaining ingredients; pour over chicken. If time permits, marinate in refrigerator. Cook in microwave at medium setting for 15 minutes. Remove chicken from dish and reserve marinade. Cook chicken on barbecue for 10 minutes, turning often and brushing with marinade. Makes 4 servings.

COMEDY

On Saturday night, **Mike Myers** does more than just talk coffee

Saturday Night Live's Mike Myers (known to viewers for such characters as metal-head Wayne Campbell of "Wayne's World" and New Yorker Linda Richman of "Coffee Talk") is the first to admit he's no whiz in the kitchen, though he does have his own unique specialty – a holdover from childhood: "You take a piece of bread, spread peanut butter on it, roll a banana in it and then cut it into coins. It's great."

The son of British-born parents, Myers grew up in Toronto as "a very picky eater," according to his mother. But Myers claims there was only one item he really hated: fish sticks. "No matter what cheery tone of voice my mom used to trick us – 'Kids! It's a treat today! Fish sticks!' I still can't eat them to this day."

Moving to New York in 1988, Myers expanded his culinary world to more exotic tastes by sampling the wide selection of ethnic foods the city has to offer. "I like Middle Eastern food – like falafel and hummus – best of all."

When Myers comes back to Toronto for a visit, his mother always spoils him by preparing trifle for dessert ("Nobody in the world can make trifle like my mother") or his favorite, Apple Fritters.

APPLE FRITTERS

1-1/3 cups	all-purpose flour	325 mL
1 tbsp	granulated sugar	15 mL
2 tsp	baking powder	10 mL
1/2 tsp	salt	2 mL
2	eggs, beaten	2
2/3 cup	milk	150 mL
1 tbsp	vegetable oil	15 mL
4 to 6	apples	4 to 6
	Oil for deep frying	
	Granulated sugar	

In bowl, stir together flour, sugar, baking powder and salt. In separate bowl, beat together eggs, milk and oil; stir into dry ingredients, mixing just until moistened. Let stand for 30 minutes. Peel and core apples. Cut into 1/3-inch (1 cm) rounds. Dip apple slices in batter. Deep fry in hot oil 375°F (190°C) for 3 to 4 minutes or until brown, turning once. Drain on paper towels. Sprinkle with sugar. Makes about 4 servings.

COMEDY

Don Ferguson takes out all the bones for an easy slice of turkey

Now in a second TV season with fellow *Royal Canadian Air Farce* troupers Roger Abbott, Luba Goy and John Morgan, Don Ferguson admits he's been involved in his share of turkeys.

So naturally there's nothing more satisfying to him than his Thanksgiving dinner ritual – boning an entire bird. "You don't need a team of chefs," he says. "You need somebody who has failed surgery." This recipe is not for the fainthearted, but Ferguson says, "What's great is that it slices like a loaf afterward."

If you have a bone to pick with Ferguson over this daring recipe, blame the Italians. A native of Montreal, Ferguson got his first taste of Italian cuisine in his late 20s. This dish is from Milan, says Ferguson, where they eat more rice than pasta. So for his family's Thanksgiving dinner in Toronto, he serves a plain risotto with the turkey.

BONELESS STUFFED TURKEY

11 lb	turkey	5 kg
1/2 lb	lean sliced bacon, parboiled (chop half into small pieces)	250 g
3/4 lb	Italian sausage removed from casing	375 g
1-3/4 lb	roasted chestnuts, cut into large pieces	875 g
14 oz	pitted prunes, coarsely chopped	400 g
2	apples, peeled and sliced	2
2	pears, peeled and sliced	2
6 tbsp	brandy	90 mL
	Salt and pepper	

The goal is to bone the turkey, without breaking the skin. Working from inside the cavity with a sharp knife, remove the wing and leg bones. Then remove the rest of the skeleton. (If this is too difficult, open the back of the turkey for access to all the bones; when done, sew or skewer the back closed.) In mixing bowl, combine chopped bacon, sausage meat, chestnuts, prunes, apple, pear and brandy. Mix well, season with salt and pepper, and use to stuff the turkey. Cover turkey breast with remaining slices of bacon, holding them in place with skewers. Roast in 350°F (180°C) oven for about 3 hours. Twenty minutes before turkey is done, remove bacon slices and baste with drippings for a nice color. The turkey should be sliced like a loaf of bread. Makes 10 to 12 servings.

 **COMEDY**

In **Meshach Taylor**'s world, his cuisine is Cajun-Creole and his spices always mixed

"I had an incredible time in Vancouver," exclaimed Meshach Taylor (Shel on *Dave's World*), who in 1993 was in B.C. appearing in a TV-movie. "The city has an incredible mixture of cuisines. You can get anything you want."

A creative cook and extensive traveller, Taylor has often tried to duplicate the dishes he has encountered on his journeys. His first love, though, remains Cajun or Creole.

Raised in New Orleans, Taylor was taught the Cajun style of cooking by his mother. His Cajun-Creole Shrimp recipe is a favorite. "I love spices but this style of food doesn't have to be spicy-hot to be successful. Spicy doesn't mean hot. Spicy means spicy. It's the mixture of spices that's important – and yes, it can be a little on the warm side if you want it to be."

CAJUN-CREOLE SHRIMP

1 lb	raw shrimp	500 g
1 tbsp	all-purpose flour	15 mL
2 tbsp	butter	25 mL
2 tbsp	tomato paste	25 mL
1	small onion, chopped	1
1/2 tsp	salt	2 mL
1/2 tsp	thyme	2 mL
1/2 to 1 tsp	red pepper flakes	2 to 5 mL
1 tbsp	chopped parsley	15 mL
1-1/4 cups	chicken broth	300 mL
3	bay leaves	3

Wash shrimp under cold water, removing shells but leaving tails on; devein shrimp. In small skillet over medium heat, cook flour until it turns light golden brown, about 5 minutes. In saucepan, melt butter and blend in flour. Stir in tomato paste, onion, salt, thyme, pepper flakes and parsley. Add broth, stirring until blended. Add bay leaves. Bring to boil, then reduce heat to simmer. Add shrimp and cook for 5 to 10 minutes or until shrimp turn pink and are just cooked through. Remove bay leaves. Serve over rice. Makes 4 servings.

PHOTO: EDDIE GARCIA/SHOOTING STAR

COMEDY

Joe Flaherty may be a maniac in the kitchen but his love of Italian cooking is no joke

For all the comic versatility he displayed on *Maniac Mansion*, Joe Flaherty is the first to admit that his creative juices run a little dry in the kitchen. "One of these days, I want to book one of those wonderful trips where you can take immersion cooking classes in Italy or France."

But in the meantime, Flaherty is known for his huge appetite, which he credits to growing up in Pittsburgh under the influence of an Italian mother and Irish father.

"My mother loved to cook and bake. So did my Italian grandmother; I remember her making big Sunday dinners, and, on holidays, ravioli and all sorts of special cookies." His Irish father was more down to basics: "He could have baked beans and boiled beef and be in heaven."

PENNONI AL TONNO

1/4 cup	olive oil	50 mL
1/2 cup	chopped onions	125 mL
3	cans (about 7 oz/200 g each) tuna packed in olive oil	3
1	can (about 1.75 oz/50 g) flat anchovies, drained and chopped	1
1	can (5-1/2 oz/156 mL) tomato paste	1
1-1/2 cups	tomato juice	375 mL
2	cloves garlic, minced	2
1 lb	pennoni, penne or tube pasta	500 g
1-1/2 cups	grated Parmesan cheese	375 mL

In large skillet, heat oil. Add onion and cook until softened. Add tuna and anchovies; stir for 2 to 3 minutes. Add tomato paste, tomato juice and garlic; stir well. Simmer uncovered for 15 minutes. Meanwhile, in large pot of boiling salted water, cook pasta until tender but firm. Drain and put in warm bowl. Add sauce; mix well. Add grated Parmesan cheese, toss and serve in heated dishes. Makes about 6 servings.

Flaherty's appreciation for Italian cooking remains today – as evidenced in his recipe for Pennoni al Tonno. But he adds one more essential ingredient: opera. "You must play Pavarotti while you cook."

COMEDY

Pam Stone gets some culinary coaching on the side to keep her in the game

Pam Stone (Judy Watkins on *Coach*) comes from a family in which her mother is English, her father is German, and they all settled in Georgia. "It's a little like *Brideshead Revisited* meets *Hogan's Heroes* meets *Mayberry, R.F.D.*," says Stone. "If you grew up with a choice of bland English steak-and-kidney pies, lumpy German-style potatoes or Southern chicken-fried steak, you'd know why food was not a priority in my life." Stone says she can eat anything without gaining a pound. But she can also "lapse into a lot of dumb habits."

Stone admits, "I can eat a chocolate cake in one sitting." But with the help of boyfriend, writer and stand-up comic Paul Zimmerman, she maintains a fairly healthy diet and a sense of humor. "He cooks and I try to irritate him."

At their home in West Hollywood, Zimmerman prepares nutritious and tasty dishes for Stone. One of her favorites is a vegetable casserole that Zimmerman named in honor of Stone. He calls it "Pam's Save-Me-From-Myself Zucchini and Corn Casserole."

ZUCCHINI AND CORN CASSEROLE

2 tbsp	vegetable oil	25 mL
1	onion, chopped	1
1	clove garlic, minced	1
4	medium zucchinis, cubed	4
2 cups	corn kernels (frozen or canned)	500 mL
1 cup	salsa	250 mL
	Salt and pepper to taste	
1 cup	shredded Monterey Jack cheese	250 mL

In skillet, heat oil. Add onion and garlic; cook until softened. Combine with zucchini, corn, salsa, salt and pepper. Pour into greased 6-cup (1.5 L) casserole dish. Sprinkle top with shredded Monterey Jack cheese. Bake in 350°F (180°C) oven for about 30 minutes or until bubbly. Makes 6 to 8 servings.

 **COMEDY**

Vegetarian **Joe Regalbuto** may order a burger at Phil's, but at home it's pass the pasta

As *Murphy Brown*'s junk-food loving, ace TV reporter Frank Fontana, Joe Regalbuto – a vegetarian since 1969 – is the first one to go for the grease at Phil's Bar. "When Frank says, 'Give me a hamburger and fries,' I always make sure there's some coleslaw on the plate, so that's what I eat when the cameras are on me." At home, Regalbuto and his wife and three children enjoy meatless Italian-style cooking; Eggplant Parmesan is a favorite. As for eating out, it's certainly a lot easier than it used to be, he says.

"You can pretty much go anywhere – from China to India – and get a vegetarian meal. I even went to a restaurant in Rome, told them we were vegetarian and, before you knew it, there were eight incredible dishes on our table."

Although he says he can relate to the insecurities of his character on *Murphy Brown*, Regalbuto is notably self-confident when it comes to what he claims is his unparalleled recipe for pesto. So passionate is he, in fact, that he has named his personal corporation, Pesto Productions, in homage. Says Regalbuto: "People *think* they make good pesto until they come to my house."

LINGUINE WITH PESTO

2 cups	fresh basil leaves	500 mL
1/2 cup	extra virgin olive oil	125 mL
6 to 8	cloves garlic, pressed	6 to 8
3/4 cup	freshly grated Parmesan cheese	175 mL
1/4 cup	pine nuts	50 mL
1 lb	fresh linguine	500 g
	Freshly ground pepper	
1	sweet red pepper, sliced	1

In blender, mix together basil and olive oil (thickness should be like pancake batter). Blend in garlic, Parmesan and pine nuts. In large pot of boiling salted water, cook linguine until al dente (tender but firm); drain. Pour pesto over pasta. Top with freshly ground pepper to taste and garnish with red pepper. Makes 3 to 4 servings.

COMEDY

Boston's **Bull & Finch Pub** cheers classic pub fare

Although *Cheers* has ended its 11-year run, the staff of the Bull & Finch Pub (the Boston watering hole that inspired the series) isn't fretting. "As long as the show is in syndication, it will still be a blessing for us," says the pub's general manager Bill Honeycutt. "It's been the greatest advertisement imaginable."

While visitors to the pub won't hear Carla razzing the customers, *Cheers* fans will immediately feel at home. The exterior of the Bull & Finch has appeared in the opening shot of the sitcom since it began in 1982, and the set was designed using the pub's interior details, with an identical door and Tiffany lamps. Only the bar is different: While Sam and Woody stand behind an island setup, the Bull & Finch mixologists work behind a cozy wall bar.

The pub's back room is where the serious eating takes place. Though it specializes in burgers, chilies and chowders, the holiday menus are also crowd pleasers.

CORNED BEEF AND CABBAGE

2-1/2 lbs	corned beef brisket	1.25 kg
	Water or chicken stock	
2	bay leave	2
	Oregano, thyme, mustard seeds, whole cloves	
1	head cabbage	1
5	potatoes	5
1-1/2 lbs	turnips	750 g
1 lb	carrots	500 g
1	small onion, quartered	1

Place corned beef in a pot and add water or chicken stock to almost cover. Add bay leaves, a large pinch of oregano and thyme, and a few mustard seeds and whole cloves. Cover and simmer, about 3 hours or until tender. Meanwhile, cut cabbage in wedges, leaving some core in each to keep their shape. Cut potatoes, turnips and carrots into 2-inch (5 cm) cubes; add to pot for last 20 to 30 minutes of cooking time. Add cabbage and onion for last 5 to 10 minutes; cook until tender. Serve with mustard, horseradish and a cold ale or dry chardonnay. Makes 4 "Norm"-sized portions.

"We do Thanksgiving and Christmas up big, and we stretch St. Patrick's Day to five days," says Honeycutt. For the Irish event, a drop of green food coloring is splashed into every brewsky, but the Corned Beef and Cabbage is classic all the way.

CELEBRITY COOKBOOK **79**

COMEDY

Rebecca Schull prefers to cook at home because she gets to wing it

Long before she was working the ticket counter on *Wings*, Rebecca Schull was a full-time mother of three who took a keen interest in her family's nutrition. "My mother, a Russian immigrant, was a dietitian, so I grew up eating well-balanced meals and I made sure my children did, too," says Schull. Today, Schull divides her time between New York and Los Angeles, where most meals on the Paramount lot include "lovely spreads of smoked salmon, bagels and fruit" and stylish, catered lunches.

On Thursdays, which is taping day, "they give us things with lots of calories," she says. But off the job, Schull prefers her cooking to any upscale cuisine. "I like to get fresh fish from the Farmer's Market in Hollywood and prepare it very simply with a vegetable." When her children visit, Schull says she fixes an old family standby that is "a meal in itself and everyone still loves" – Cabbage Borscht.

CABBAGE BORSCHT

2 lbs	beef brisket	1 kg
1	marrow bone	1
1	onion, diced	1
2 cups	canned tomatoes	500 mL
1	medium cabbage, shredded	1
1/2 cup	raisins	125 mL
	Juice of 2 lemons	
1/4 cup	brown sugar (or to taste)	50 mL
2 tsp	salt	10 mL
	Pepper to taste	

Place meat and marrow bone in large pot; add 6 cups (1.5 L) water. Bring to rapid boil; skim. Add onion and tomatoes. Bring to boil, then reduce heat; cover and simmer until meat is tender, about 2 hours. Meanwhile, sprinkle shredded cabbage with a handful of salt and let stand while soup is cooking. Rinse cabbage with hot water and drain; add to soup. Add raisins. Cover and simmer, about 30 minutes, or until cabbage is tender. Add lemon juice, sugar, salt and pepper. Simmer for 10 minutes longer. Makes about 8 servings.

SOAPS Off the air, soap stars are really cookin', too

Victoria Rowell steams up salmon in her kitchen

Victoria Rowell is enjoying a double dose of the Hollywood limelight – appearing as both Drucilla Winters in *The Young and the Restless* and Amanda Bentley in *Diagnosis Murder* – but her taste in food is entirely down to earth. Growing up on a 60-acre farm in Maine made her "self-sufficient," she says.

"We harvested squash, corn, tomatoes, strawberries, rhubarb, pumpkins and beets. Everything was natural and organic. It was really clean living."

And Rowell continues her clean living today, sticking to simply prepared, healthful foods like her show-stopping Steamed Salmon, which was inspired by singer-songwriter James Taylor.

"I was invited to a party at his home," recalls Rowell, "and he made the most incredible seafood stew. He took a corrugated barrel and put seaweed and beer in it, and sausage and seafood. He let it steam and, when it was through cooking, he dumped it directly onto a picnic table and we feasted on it."

STEAMED SALMON

4	salmon fillets (about 4 oz/125 g each)	4
2 tbsp	vegetable oil	25 mL
2	cloves garlic, minced	2
1 cup	soy sauce	250 mL
1/4 tsp	pepper	1 mL
1/4 tsp	thyme	1 mL
2 tsp	rosemary	10 mL
8	new potatoes, halved	8
1	onion, diced	1
16	cherrystone clams in shell, cleaned	16
1 tbsp	chopped fresh basil	15 mL

Place salmon in large shallow dish. Combine oil, garlic, soy sauce, pepper, thyme and rosemary; pour over salmon; marinate in refrigerator up to 1 hour. Parboil potatoes for 10 minutes; set aside. After fish has marinated, place each fillet on large sheet of aluminum foil. Top fillets with potatoes, onions, clams and basil. Gather foil up around each fillet, sealing loosely but completely. Bake in 350°F (180°C) oven for 35 minutes or until salmon flakes with a fork and potatoes are tender. Serve with corn. Makes 4 servings.

SOAPS

Bobbie Eakes chooses low-cal food but loves Southern cooking

"Mega-calories! Southern cooking is loaded with them, so I try to stay away from those foods. But they're so good!" says Bobbie Eakes in a Southern drawl. "When I make my mom's recipe for Georgia Pecan Pie, I serve a pork roast that you slow-cook on the barbecue all day long, with all the fixin's like fried okra and cornbread."

But for everyday eating, Eakes, who plays Macy on *The Bold and the Beautiful*, says, "I'm much more apt to make a pasta with a tomato-basil sauce to keep down the calories."

The youngest of five daughters born to an Air Force family, the former Miss Georgia says, "I enjoy cooking, but not necessarily Southern cooking. My mom has all these great recipes, but they're time consuming and I'm not really into elaborate entertaining."

Eakes enjoys cooking for small groups of friends "more on the casual side." With a hectic schedule of acting plus a singing career (she and *B&B* costar Jeff Trachta have released an album in Europe), she says her favorite kitchen appliance besides the dishwasher is "the food processor. I have lots of gadgets and gizmos to save time."

GEORGIA PECAN PIE

3	eggs	3
1 cup	brown sugar	250 mL
1 cup	light corn syrup	250 mL
1-1/2 tbsp	butter, melted	20 mL
1 tsp	vanilla	5 mL
1/4 tsp	salt	1 mL
2 tbsp	all-purpose flour	25 mL
2 cups	pecan halves	500 mL
1	unbaked pastry shell (9 inch/23 cm)	1
	Whipped cream	

In large bowl, combine eggs, brown sugar, syrup, butter, vanilla and salt; beat until frothy. Stir in flour; mix well. Stir in pecans. Pour into pastry shell. Bake in 350°F (180°C) oven for 35 minutes or until set. Let cool. To serve, top with whipped cream. Makes 6 to 8 servings.

SOAPS

Betty Driver can dish it up at the Rovers, but would she eat the food?

Many *Coronation Street* regulars find themselves in the Rovers pub come lunchtime when the specialty of the house – Betty Turpin's famous hearty Hotpot – is the favorite accompaniment to the usual liquid refreshment.

Actress Betty Driver, playing Betty Turpin, has been serving up the popular Lancashire dish for 25 years on the show but, when asked what kind of food the *real* Betty likes, she says, "Any kind. I love Italian, Jewish, French, Chinese, you name it."

Driver includes chicken and fish in her diet but, ironically, avoids red meat. So does that mean she wouldn't eat her own Hotpot? She laughs, "Er, no…but I might make a Chicken Hotpot! Can you imagine it in the Rovers? That would be nice. We'll have to have a go at that!"

CORONATION STREET HOTPOT

2 tbsp	each: dripping and butter (or 1/4 cup/50 mL butter)	25 mL
1-1/2 lbs	neck of lamb cubed, or lamb shoulder chops	750 g
2	onions, coarsely chopped	2
1 tbsp	flour	15 mL
1-3/4 cups	light stock or hot water	425 mL
1 tbsp	Worcestershire sauce	15 mL
	Salt and pepper	
1	bay leaf	1
1-1/2 lbs	potatoes, peeled and thinly sliced	750 g

In heavy skillet over high heat, melt 2 tbsp (25 mL) dripping and butter. Fry the meat until nicely browned. Remove meat from pan and place in deep casserole. Reduce heat to medium. Fry onions in pan juices, adding a little more butter or dripping if necessary. When onions are soft and starting to brown, stir in flour. Gradually stir in stock or water. Bring to simmer, stirring constantly; add Worcestershire sauce and salt and pepper to taste. Pour onions and liquid over meat; mix well. Tuck in bay leaf. Arrange potatoes in overlapping layers over meat, seasoning each layer with salt and pepper. Dot top layer of potato with remainder of butter. Cover and cook in 325°F (160°C) oven for 2 hours. Uncover and cook for 30 minutes longer. If potatoes are not brown, increase oven temperature and cook for 15 minutes longer. Makes 4 servings.

SOAPS

Susan Lucci married a chef for food and romance in real life

The way to Susan Lucci's heart was through her taste buds, so it's no surprise that 24 years later she's still married to Austrian-trained chef Helmut Huber (even though she's become famous playing the tempestuous Erica Kane on *All My Children* for as long as she's been married). While other suitors tried for her hand with flowers and promises of the good life, Huber, now a businessman, won her over dinner, talking food.

"I've always loved to eat," says Lucci, "but I was rather like the person who says about a painting, 'I don't know much about art, but I know what I like.' I hadn't realized how much I was missing by not knowing more about food and cooking."

In the kitchen of their palatial Georgian townhouse on Long Island, Lucci, 44 (who has a college-age daughter and teenage son), likes to cook for guests whenever her schedule permits. An all-Susan menu includes chilled avocado soup, stuffed veal rolls and strawberry sherbet. Or for a more intimate occasion like a fireside supper for two, this seductively smooth cheese fondue is a favorite.

FIRESIDE FONDUE

1 tbsp	butter	15 mL
1 cup	white wine	250 mL
1/2 lb	Swiss (Emmenthal) cheese, shredded	250 g
1/2 lb	Gruyère cheese, shredded	250 g
1 tbsp	cornstarch	15 mL
1/2 tsp	salt	2 mL
1/4 tsp	black pepper	1 mL
Pinch	grated nutmeg	Pinch
1 tbsp	brandy	15 mL
	French bread, cut into large cubes	

In fondue pot, melt butter; tilt to coat inner surface of pot. Pour in wine and let it warm. In bowl, combine cheeses, cornstarch, salt, pepper and nutmeg; mix thoroughly. Add cheese mixture by the handful to wine, stirring until smooth after each addition. Stir in brandy. Place fondue pot over adjustable flame. With fondue forks, dip bread cubes into cheese mixture. Makes about 6 servings.

PHOT: EDIE BASKIN/ONYX

 **SOAPS**

John Aprea, in true Italian style, likes a full house of dinner guests

"Italian sons don't spend that much time in the kitchen," admits John Aprea. "But what I do cook, I cook fairly well. Maybe it's in the genes."

Commuting between New York and Los Angeles when he played reformed bad guy Lucas on *Another World* and John Stamos's father on the sitcom *Full House*, Aprea's schedule left little time for cooking.

But he says, "I like to dabble in the kitchen when I can; cooking is relaxing to me." He says he cooked more in L.A. than in New York. "My wife and I enjoy entertaining, especially when you get 10 or 12 people together, all talking and eating at the same time."

Born in New Jersey to immigrant Italian parents, Aprea worked summers in his family's produce store. And not surprisingly, his forte is mostly Italian recipes handed down through the generations. "But you know Italians," he says. "If you want a recipe, they tell you to put in 'a little of this, a little of that.' You figure it out by watching, which is how I learned from my mother. But even she doesn't do all those heavy meat dishes any more. Tastes have changed. Now it's mostly fast and light sauces."

PASTA SORRENTO

1/2 cup	olive oil	125 mL
4	cloves garlic, minced	4
2-1/2 cups	crushed tomatoes, with juice	625 mL
	Salt and pepper	
	Red pepper flakes	
1/4 cup	anchovies, drained	50 mL
1/4 cup	capers	50 mL
1 cup	black olives, pitted and sliced	250 mL
1 lb	linguine	500 g

In large skillet, heat oil. Add garlic; cook until golden. Add tomatoes; simmer for 10 to 15 minutes. Add salt, pepper and red pepper to taste. Add anchovies and capers; simmer for 5 minutes longer. Add olives. Meanwhile, in large pot of boiling salted water, cook linguine until al dente (tender but firm). Drain and toss with sauce. Makes 4 servings.

 **SOAPS**

These days, **Matthew Ashford** tips his cap to healthy eating

Matthew Ashford, who played devilish Jack Devereaux on *Days of Our Lives*, admits he's no killer in the kitchen. "When I got married, I came with a dowry of assorted cooking pots; however, the extent of my expertise was limited to making popcorn in the large one."

Fortunately, Ashford's wife, actress Christina Saffran, introduced him to the other pots and pans when the couple moved into their 60-year-old L.A. home.

"And we keep our kitchen stocked with cookbooks of every kind. If we were to throw a party tonight, we'd probably prepare salad, pasta – I love making pasta – and a skinless chicken dish."

Ashford says he only recently realized that good eating habits and exercise are very important and reflect on how you generally feel.

"So I'm learning to make more nutritious food now – low fat, low salt – a challenge for a popcorn addict. But I enjoy hearty, healthy meals that include lots of vegetables. And I really like this mushroom recipe that's been in the family for years."

STUFFED MUSHROOMS

20	medium-sized mushrooms	20
1	small onion	1
1/2 tsp	salt	2 mL
1/2 tsp	pepper	2 mL
6 tbsp	butter	90 mL
6	slices white bread, crusts removed	6
1/2 cup	freshly grated Parmesan cheese	125 mL
	Chopped parsley	

Remove mushroom stems; chop and set aside. Place mushroom caps, top down, on baking sheet. In skillet, heat butter; sauté onions and mushroom stems until onion is softened. Cut bread into coarse crumbs (in food processor if desired). Add bread crumbs and Parmesan to skillet. Remove pan from heat and stir until crumbs absorb butter. Spoon mixture into mushroom caps. Bake in 400°F (200°C) oven for about 10 minutes or until browned on top. Sprinkle with chopped parsley. Makes 4 to 6 servings.

SOAPS

Eileen Fulton's world turns around healthy food in her kitchen

For over two decades, Eileen Fulton has been wreaking havoc as the manipulative Lisa on *As the World Turns*. But she says, "We really aren't much alike."

Lisa would never be found donning an apron because she owns her own restaurant, says Fulton, who professes to being a fine cook herself. "My mother and grandmother were excellent cooks, especially when it came to making great biscuits and cornbread," says the North Carolina native. The kitchen in her New York apartment is compact, but the one in her Connecticut home boasts a large cooking area and "on my windowsill, I have this teeny herb garden which I absolutely love."

CORNBREAD

2 cups	all-purpose flour	500 mL
1-1/2 cups	cornmeal	375 mL
1/4 cup	granulated sugar	50 mL
1 tbsp	baking powder	15 mL
1 tsp	baking soda	5 mL
1 tsp	salt	5 mL
4	eggs	4
1-1/2 cups	buttermilk	375 mL
1	can (14 oz/398 mL) creamed corn	1
1/2 cup	melted butter	125 mL

In bowl, mix together flour, cornmeal, sugar, baking powder, baking soda and salt. In another bowl, whisk together eggs, buttermilk, corn and butter. Add to dry ingredients, mixing just until combined. Pour into greased 12 x 8-inch (3 L) baking dish. Bake in 375°F (190°C) oven for 35 to 40 minutes or until tester inserted in centre comes out clean. Let cool on rack. Cut into squares.

Says Fulton, "I eat what's healthy, such as chicken, pasta, rice and vegetables, or I mix up a great breakfast shake from bananas, strawberries and skim milk."

Fulton's cooking habits reflect her philosophy on aging. "I think it's very important to take care of yourself, which means eating the right foods. But I don't dwell on getting older, just as I don't constantly think about what I cook for myself."

SOAPS

High-roller **Thom Christopher** practises economy in the kitchen

Growing up in New York was something of a feast for Thom Christopher, whose mother, Nancy, "was the most incredible Italian cook. What always fascinated me about my mom was that she could work all day, come home and unexpectedly cook for 20 people." Today, Christopher (a Daytime Emmy Award winner for his role as drug kingpin Carlo Hesser, transformed into jewel expert Mortimer Bern on *One Life to Live*) enjoys throwing his own elaborate dinner parties in his Manhattan townhouse.

His wife, Judy, creates the main courses while he whips up the appetizers and desserts. His recipe for sautéed vegetables – which can be served as an appetizer or a side dish – reflects his cooking philosophy. "I believe in economy in the kitchen," he says. "You can eat very nicely without spending a lot."

WOK VEGETABLES

2 tbsp	sesame oil	25 mL
1/4 lb	broccoli florets	125 g
2	carrots, sliced	2
12	asparagus tips	12
1	small zucchini, sliced	1
1/4 lb	snow peas	125 g
1	small red onion sliced	1,
1/4 lb	mushrooms	125 g
1	each: red and yellow pepper, julienned	1
1 lb	tofu, cubed (optional)	500g
	Tamari, peanut or soy sauce	

Heat wok or deep frying pan until very hot; coat inside with sesame oil. Add broccoli, carrots and asparagus; cook, stirring often, for a few minutes. Then add zucchini, snow peas, onions, mushrooms and peppers; cook, stirring, for another minute or two. If you like tofu, add and cook for 2 more minutes. Add sauce to taste. Continue cooking, stirring frequently, until vegetables are tender but not overcooked. Makes about 8 servings.

CHEFS Masters of the kitchen share recipes for success

Continental **Martin Yan** has something new cooking and so can you

Everybody thinks *Yan Can Cook* is a Canadian production – and that's fine with me!" laughs internationally renowned chef Martin Yan, who launched his popular cooking show in Calgary 16 years ago (it later moved to Toronto before settling in San Francisco).

"There is tremendous respect for Canadians in China. When I go there and pull out my Canadian passport, they love it!" And lately, he's been passing through those portals frequently. Yan has been filming throughout China and will use the footage to jazz up his 1995 season.

Shows will spotlight all types of regional Chinese cuisine including a dish he found in Northern China. "There is a very simple dish with a cooked meat patty that is put inside a bun, almost like a pita bread. It is a tradition thousands of years old – one on which I based my recipe for Asian Burgers," he says. While the recipe incorporates textures and tastes that may take traditional hamburger lovers aback, Yan promises that everyone will *love* it!

ASIAN BURGERS

1 lb	lean ground beef	500 g
1/4 lb	firm tofu (drained, squeezed, dried in cheesecloth), crumbled	125 g
1/2	medium onion, chopped	1/2
4	green onions, chopped	4
3 tbsp	ground, toasted sesame seeds	50 mL
3 tbsp	soy sauce	50 mL
1 tbsp	coarsely chopped cilantro	15 mL
2 tsp	sesame oil	10 mL
1/2 tsp	salt	2 mL
2 tsp	cornstarch	10 mL
6	hamburger buns (or 4 pita breads, halved)	6

Condiments: kim chee, cilantro, green onions, hoisin sauce or your favorite condiments

Combine patty ingredients; mix well. Divide mixture into 6 equal portions; lightly shape each portion into a patty. (For pita bread, make 8 smaller patties.) Cook patties on an oiled grill, about 3 minutes on each side for medium rare. Makes 4 to 6 servings.

CHEFS

The grande dame of French cuisine
Julia Child keeps on cooking

Even if she didn't stand 6-foot-2, chef Julia Child would still be head and shoulders above the culinary crowd. At a lively age 81, the legendary television chef and "grande dame" of cuisine in North America came out with her latest TV series and companion book – "Cooking with Master Chefs" (Knopf, 1994). Designed for the average but serious cook, the series has Child visiting American chefs in their home kitchens.

Child's popular TV cooking shows began with WGBH Boston's *The French Chef* in 1963. Lately, she has been working on two more seasons of her latest series, *In Julia's Kitchen with Master Chefs*, which will debut in '95.

Child believes all culinary effort should bring pleasure at the table. "I believe in enjoying every mouthful." When she discovered that her audience's all-time favorite dish is Chocolate Mousse, she devised this extra-easy recipe which is taken from her book "The Way to Cook" (Knopf, 1989). With a wink, she advises, "Call it Chocolate Ganache Coupé; that sounds classier."

CHOCOLATE MOUSSE

8 oz	sweet or semisweet baking chocolate	240 g
1/4 cup	strong coffee	50 mL
6 tbsp	softened, unsalted butter	90 mL
3	egg yolks	3
1 cup	whipping cream	250 mL
3	egg whites	3
1/4 cup	superfine sugar	50 mL

In heavy saucepan over low heat, melt chocolate in coffee. Beat soft butter smoothly into melted chocolate. Beat in egg yolks, one at a time. Whip cream; set aside. In bowl, beat egg whites until they hold soft peaks; then, while beating, sprinkle in sugar by spoonfuls and continue beating until whites hold stiff peaks. Add chocolate mixture to one side of egg whites in bowl and fold them together. When almost blended, fold in whipped cream. Turn mousse into serving bowl or individual containers. Cover and chill several hours. Garnish with whipped cream, if desired. Makes 6 to 8 servings.

PHOTO: AARON RAPOPORT/ONYX

CHEFS

Bonnie Stern is enthusiastic about cooking on camera and off

"A lot of people view cooking as work," says Toronto cooking-school owner and cookbook author Bonnie Stern. "I like to make it easier and more fun," she says. And Stern always looks like she's having fun on her appearances on CTV's *Canada AM*.

She says she loves live TV because there's always the element of chance – like the morning the food processor didn't work and she had to talk her way through a demonstration. "Cooking on television is a cross between scary and exciting," she says. "But I love anything to do with food and want to make other people enjoy it, too."

Off camera, Stern shares her enthusiasm through her cooking school, newspaper columns and cookbooks. Her latest book, "Simply HeartSmart Cooking" (Random House, 1994), features light recipes including Ricotta Bruschetta, a creative start to any gathering. "When you entertain, the first thing you serve is an appetizer. It's your first chance to influence guests," she says. "An appealing appetizer makes people hungry for more food. It doesn't matter if it's simple or fancy as long as it's good quality."

RICOTTA BRUSCHETTA

1 lb	light ricotta cheese	500 g
1	thin French stick (about 16 inches/40 cm)	1
1/2 tsp	pepper	2 mL
2 tbsp	chopped fresh parsley	25 mL
2 tbsp	chopped fresh chives or green onions	25 mL
2 tbsp	chopped fresh basil or dill	25 mL
1 tbsp	chopped fresh mint (or 1/4 tsp/1mL dried)	15 mL
2 tbsp	olive oil (optional)	25 mL
1/4 tsp	hot red pepper flakes	1 mL
2	cloves garlic, minced	2
	Salt to taste	

If ricotta is watery, cut in quarters, place in strainer and allow to drain for a few hours. Slice bread on diagonal into 1/2-inch (1 cm) slices. Arrange in single layer on baking sheets. Preheat broiler and broil until slightly crusty on each side but still a little soft in centre. Place ricotta in bowl and beat in pepper, parsley, chives, basil and mint. Add olive oil, hot pepper flakes, garlic and salt. Spread each piece of bread with about 4 tsp (20 mL) ricotta mixture. Makes about 24 appetizers.

CHEFS

Entertaining guru **Martha Stewart** keeps the traditional Easter spirit alive

The trouble with the world today is "we've forgotten about tradition," says Martha Stewart, who has become a household name by specializing in absolutely everything relating to the home. "It's so important to keep tradition alive, and to keep tradition alive, you have to do it at home." Stewart is a best-selling author of books on cooking, weddings, entertaining, decorating and gardening, and she's also the host of her own syndicated TV show, *Martha Stewart Living*.

Stewart helps to keep the spirit of Easter alive by preparing the same kind of traditional Polish-style Easter Sunday brunch that her mother and grandmother used to make.

"When I was growing up, the priest from our church came to visit on Saturday, so we had to get a lot of the cooking done ahead of time. Baked ham, scalloped potatoes, colored hard-boiled eggs, and macaroni with cheese can all be done in advance. The only thing I make on Sunday is a fresh green salad."

To decorate her Easter table, Stewart uses satin ribbon to suspend colored eggs over the table. "I also like to surround the ham with fresh pea vines, and I line wicker baskets with moss and mound eggs up in the baskets."

BAKED EASTER HAM

8 to 10 lb	uncooked smoked ham, bone-in	4 to 5 kg
1/2 cup	Dijon mustard with whole seeds	125 mL
1 cup	apricot jam	250 mL
1/4 cup	dry sherry	50 mL

Line baking pan with foil. Place ham, fat side up, on foil. Wrap well with another piece of foil. Bake in 275°F (140°C) oven for 2-1/2 to 3 hours. Remove from oven; remove foil wrapping. With large sharp knife, cut off rind and all but 1/4 inch (5 mm) of fat. Score fat in diamond pattern. For glaze, combine mustard, jam and sherry. Pour out any pan juices. Lightly coat ham with glaze and return it to oven. Bake for 1 hour, spooning more of glaze over ham every 15 minutes. Remove to serving platter. Makes 10 to 12 servings.

CHEFS

Kids love cooking and eating in **Pam Collacott**'s kitchen

As host of the "Pam's Kitchen" segment on YTV's *Take Part*, Pam Collacott demonstrates how much fun cooking with children can be – with an emphasis on safety and nutrition. A former home economics teacher who runs her own cooking school near Ottawa, Collacott developed many of her teaching techniques while raising her own two children. "Giving them easy things to do, like stirring sauce, measuring ingredients or chopping bananas – with a dull knife, of course – not only got them involved but also got things done a lot quicker I found."

Collacott also teaches and writes a newspaper column on microwave cooking and is author of "The Best of New Wave Cooking" (Creative Bound, 1992), which includes a selection of easy recipes for young cooks. Her earlier cookbook for kids, "Pam's Kitchen" (Macmillan, 1990), is filled with child-tested recipes. Here are three ideas for cute animal salads that little kids love to make and to eat.

ANIMAL SALADS

Place lettuce leaf on plate and assemble a Bunny, Mousey or Spider on top. (Use small toothpicks to hold pieces that won't stick.)

BUNNY
Body: 1 pear half
Nose: 1 piece of cherry (at narrow end)
Eyes: 2 raisins (just above nose)
Ears: 2 almonds (above eyes)
Tail: 1 small cauliflower floret

MOUSEY
Body: 1 pear half
Nose: 1 small piece of cherry
Eyes: 2 currants or raisin halves
Ears: 2 marshmallow slices (cut with scissors)
Tail: 1 green bean

SPIDER
Body: 1/2 tomato, round side up
Eyes: 2 slices of olive or radish
Antennae: 2 thin celery sticks
Legs: 8 carrot curls or slices
Mouth: 1 piece of green pepper

CHEFS

Marcel Desaulniers revels in bowls filled with innocent pleasure

For those who like to live dangerously, *Death by Chocolate* is a series no dessert daredevil should miss. Marcel Desaulniers – chef, author and host of the series on TLC – knows what he's talking about. "When so many of yesterday's fashionable trends and habits are today's misdemeanors, we should rejoice that a chocolate dessert can bring so much innocent pleasure."

Death by Chocolate is the name of a super-decadent chocolate cake that was created 12 years ago and still remains the favorite dessert at his Trellis Restaurant in Williamsburg, Va. The recipe and many delicious others are included in Desaulniers' "Death by Chocolate" cookbook (Random House, 1992).

With such a repertoire, Desaulniers is hard-pressed to name a favorite. "But if I had to choose one, I would say Mocha Java Sorbet. It has no butter or eggs, so I justify that to mean I can have bowls of it." Of course, it does have the one ingredient essential for all his desserts. It's "overwhelmingly chocolate!"

MOCHA JAVA SORBET

6 oz	unsweetened chocolate	180 g
2 oz	semisweet chocolate	60 g
2 cups	water	500 mL
2 cups	granulated sugar	500 mL
1-1/2 cups	strong coffee	375 mL
1 tsp	pure vanilla extract	5 mL

Break chocolate into 1/2-inch (1 cm) pieces. In saucepan over medium-high heat, combine water, sugar and coffee; whisk to dissolve sugar. Bring to boil. Place chocolate pieces in stainless steel bowl. Remove boiling liquid from heat and pour 1 cup (250 mL) over chocolate. Allow to stand for 5 minutes, then whisk vigorously until completely smooth, about 3 minutes. Add remaining hot liquid and whisk until smooth. Cool in ice water bath (40-45°F/ 5-7°C), about 20 minutes or until cold. Stir in vanilla. Freeze in ice-cream maker following manufacturer's instructions. Transfer sorbet to plastic container; place in freezer for several hours. Serve within 2 days. Makes about 8 cups (2 L).

CHEFS

Burt Wolf travels the world to bring local dishes to his kitchen

Some viewers may have been confused when they watched *Burt Wolf, Eating Well*: Was it a cooking show or was it a *National Geographic* special? That's because the series traveled around the world in search of interesting dishes. "I always tried to uncover an area's unique gastronomy," says chef-author-host Wolf.

Wolf and crew visited each region to find picture-perfect locations; two stops were in the Montreal and Quebec City regions. "I was interested in the kind of cooking that the early French settlers did – the meat pie," says Wolf. "The pies originated in a society where everyone worked very long hours. You had to get the cooking out of the way because you also had to make soap and candles and chop wood. They were always looking for dishes that got everything into one pot and would cook really slowly while they were out in the fields."

MEAT PIES

1 cup	each: diced beef, veal and chicken	250 mL
1 tbsp	each: finely chopped shallots, fresh parsley, basil, chives	15 mL
1-1/2 tsp	chopped fresh tarragon (or 3/4 tsp/3 mL dried)	7 mL
1 tsp	chopped fresh thyme (or 1/2 tsp/2 mL dried)	5 mL
	Salt and pepper to taste	
1	large potato, peeled and diced	1
1	egg, beaten	1
	Pastry to fit 6 large muffin cups and tops	

Place each cup of meat in separate bowl. Season each with shallots, herbs, salt and pepper. Line 6 large nonstick muffin cups with pastry. Fill cups with layers of meat and potato, starting with beef, then half of the potato, chicken, remaining potato and veal. Press down slightly to compress the filling. Dampen top edge of pastry shells with water; top with rounds of pastry; press edges to seal. With small knife, score edge of each pie without cutting through dough. Make a hole in centre of each so steam can escape. Brush top crust with beaten egg. Bake in 350°F (180°C) oven for 50 minutes or until well browned. Serve warm. Makes 6.

CHEFS

Laurie Burrows Grad makes light and easy work of cooking on TV

Light cooking is all the rage these days. And Laurie Burrows Grad believes it should be quick and easy, too. On her TLC series, *Laurie Cooks Light & Easy*, she breezes through the preparation of three or four light-and-easy dishes in every half-hour segment. She also has no problem finding guests for the show. In most episodes, she shares the kitchen spotlight with a celebrity cook.

With low-fat cooking at centre stage in the food world, there's no shortage of restaurant chefs, authors and other food professionals all eager to share recipes, techniques and tips.

Burrows Grad also invites many showbiz chums to cook along with her on the show, and again she has a wide network of contacts. Several of her family members are television producers, and her husband, Peter Grad, was the president of MTM.

FLUFFY LIGHT MEAT LOAF

1 lb	lean ground beef (or half beef, half veal)	500 g
3/4 cup	oatmeal	175 mL
3 tbsp	finely chopped green pepper or celery	50 mL
1	small onion, finely chopped	1
1 tbsp	finely chopped parsley	15 mL
1	can (5-1/2 oz/156 mL) tomato paste	1
1	egg, lightly beaten	1
1/4 tsp	minced garlic	1 mL
	Salt and pepper to taste	
	Chili sauce	

Combine all ingredients except chili sauce. Mixing with your hands, form into a loaf and place in 9 x 5-inch (2 L) loaf pan. Cover with layer of chili sauce. Bake in 350°F (180°C) oven for 50 to 60 minutes. Garnish with parsley sprigs or halved cherry tomatoes. Makes 3 to 4 servings.

Burrows Grad began her career writing food columns, then jumped into TV cooking on a local L.A. show with Regis Philbin. Television ties also extend to personal friends, such as *L.A. Law*'s Michael Tucker. "Jill (Eikenberry, Tucker's wife) doesn't love to cook but Michael adores it," says Burrows Grad. "We had tremendous fun doing the show. On that episode, we prepared Fluffy Meat Loaf."

CHEFS

James Barber is just an urban peasant who believes in getting down to basics

In a kitchen bursting with flowers and garlic braids, James Barber powers through preparation of a meal including gin and tomato soup and asparagus with ginger.

The essence of *The Urban Peasant* series (on CBC and TLC) is that all food is prepared in real time, which means every dish is completed from scratch in each half-hour segment. The essence of James Barber is that he likes things simple and unpretentious.

"People have gotten fed up with gourmet shows and the idea they have to measure up to someone else's standards," says the affable Barber. "Most people don't have kitchens that are immaculate. And when they cook, they make a mess and they make mistakes."

Barber is a believer in getting down to basics. "The show is about comfort food, something that will make you feel good," he says, like his Red and Yellow Pepper Stew with Anchovies. "People are realizing that cooking can be fun and not complicated. You have to relax. It's just like making love. You do the best you can with what you've got."

RED AND YELLOW PEPPER STEW WITH ANCHOVIES

2 tbsp	olive or vegetable oil	25 mL
1	onion, cut in chunks	1
1	each: red and yellow pepper, cut in chunks	1
3	cloves garlic, minced	3
3	anchovy fillets, minced	3
	Freshly ground pepper	
	Salt	
1 tbsp	vinegar	15 mL

In skillet, heat oil. Add onion, peppers and garlic. Mix in anchovies and add pepper and a sprinkling of salt (anchovies are already very salty). Cook mixture over high heat, stirring often, until peppers are tender. Stir in vinegar. Serve immediately. Makes 2 servings.

SPORTS Scoring high points with culinary inspiration

When **Ron MacLean** serves up dinner, pasta is his three-star selection

Bouncing from city to city with the Stanley Cup playoffs, CBC commentator Ron MacLean should have plenty of opportunity to sample some of the continent's finest cuisines. Wrong.

"My cohorts [Bob Cole, Harry Neale and Don Cherry] don't really like to go out and indulge in the gourmet experience, at least not as often as I'd like to," he says.

When MacLean and his pals do go out for dinner, the meal is pub fare "in a restaurant that has a satellite so we can watch hockey games."

At home in Oakville, Ont., MacLean loves to barbecue. But sometimes he'll step up to the stove and reach for "Tiger in the Kitchen: Done Like Dinner" (Douglas & McIntyre, 1987), co-written by former NHLer Tiger Williams that serves up recipes from NHL players. MacLean's favorite dish is Italian Sausage Pasta.

ITALIAN SAUSAGE PASTA

1-1/2 lbs	Italian or chorizo sausage	750 g
1/2 cup	olive oil	125 mL
1-1/2 lbs	eggplant, cubed	750 g
1	onion, chopped	1
1	green pepper, chopped	1
3	cloves garlic, minced	3
1 tsp	each: oregano, basil, thyme	5 mL
1 tsp	granulated sugar	5 mL
	Salt and pepper to taste	
1	can (28 oz/796 mL) Italian plum tomatoes	1
1/4 cup	chopped, stuffed green olives	50 mL
1 cup	dry red wine	250 mL
1-1/2 lbs	rotini or large shell pasta	750 g
1 cup	freshly grated Parmesan cheese	250 mL
1/4 cup	chopped parsley	50 mL

Remove casings from sausage. In heavy saucepan, brown sausage until crumbly; drain and transfer to bowl. In same saucepan, heat oil. Add eggplant, onion, green pepper, garlic, oregano, basil, thyme, sugar, salt and pepper; cook until eggplant is softened. Add sausage, tomatoes, olives and wine. Bring to boil, reduce heat and simmer for about 1-1/2 hours, stirring occasionally, until sauce is thickened. Meanwhile, in large pot of boiling salted water, cook pasta until tender but firm; drain. Serve topped with sauce. Sprinkle with Parmesan and parsley. Makes 6 servings.

 **SPORTS**

Wayne Gretzky's eatery serves "stick-to-the-ribs" fare

If you're going to eat at Wayne Gretzky's, you had better call ahead. The Toronto restaurant and sports bar at "99" Blue Jays Way has been packed ever since it opened in September '93.

The 270-seat eatery is proving to be uncommonly popular, partly because it's become a regular post-game stop for many sports stars – including Gretzky when the Los Angeles Kings visit Toronto. The restaurant doubles as a sort of Gretzky Hall of Fame, featuring some of the most notable artifacts – including jerseys, score sheets and record-breaking pucks – from a most notable career.

When it comes time to eat, Gretzky's offers stick-to-the-ribs fare in hearty portions. Chef Christopher Klugman arranged the menu with many of Gretzky's personal favorites in mind including hot cheese and artichoke dip and Gretzky's Great Pirogis.

PHOTO: GARY MOSS/OUTLINE PRESS

GRETZKY'S GREAT PIROGIS

1	red sweet pepper	1
1-1/2 cups	vegetables (broccoli, zucchini, etc.) in bite-size pieces	375 mL
3 tbsp	butter	50 mL
6 oz	chorizo sausage, thinly sliced	175 g
1	small onion, sliced	1
2 tsp	chopped garlic	10 mL
1 tbsp	chopped fresh herbs (rosemary, thyme, oregano)	15mL
24	pirogis, parboiled	24
1/3 cup	white wine	75 mL
1	bunch green onions, chopped	1
1 tsp	coarse black pepper	5 mL
3/4 cup	sour cream	175 mL

Broil red pepper for 5 to 10 minutes, turning occasionally, until skin is blackened. Holding pepper under cold water, peel off charred skin and remove seeds. Slice pepper into 1/4-in (5 mm) strips; set aside. Cook vegetables in boiling water until tender-crisp; set aside. In large pan over medium-high heat, combine butter, sausage, onions, garlic and fresh herbs. Cook, stirring, until onion is softened. Add pirogis and continue to cook, stirring often, until pirogis and onions are golden brown. Add reserved pepper strips and vegetables; cook for 1 minute. Add wine, green onions and pepper; cook for another minute. Remove from heat, stir in sour cream. Serves 4.

SPORTS

Don Cherry is a regular meat-and-potatoes and salmon-sandwich kinda guy

Don Cherry says he's a "meat and potatoes guy" even when more exotic fare is available on the road with CBC's *Hockey Night in Canada* crew.

"When I go out to dinner with them, they like to order dishes you can't pronounce. I like to have a nice cut of roast beef or a steak." When he's home, Cherry leaves most of the cooking to his wife, Rose. And when he's in another city with *HNIC*, he always eats the same meal: two salmon sandwiches with a slice of cheese on wholewheat bread – preferably prepared by Rose.

"When the guys go out for dinner, I stay in my room and eat those sandwiches. It stems back to my minor-league days when you didn't want to waste time eating."

But when he does eat out, it's not surprising to hear Cherry admit that he has "the typical redneck, average-guy diet: meat and potatoes." And, he adds, he still believes that "hockey players should eat meat. Rick Vaive scored 50 goals three years in a row (for the Toronto Maple Leafs in the early '80s), then he started eating nuts and lettuce and dropped to 35 goals."

Cherry's other favorite is chili. "I love chili, but it can't be too spicy."

CHERRY'S CHILI

1-1/2 lbs	lean ground beef	375 g
1	onion, chopped	1
1	green pepper, chopped	1
1	can (10 oz/284 mL) tomato soup	1
1	can (19 oz/540 mL) red kidney beans	1
2 tbsp	chili powder (or to taste)	25 mL
1/2 tsp	salt	2 mL

In skillet, combine ground beef, onion and pepper. Cook over medium-high heat, stirring frequently, for about 10 minutes, until meat begins to brown and onion is tender. Stir in tomato soup, kidney beans, chili powder and salt. Cover and simmer for 25 minutes; uncover and simmer for about 15 minutes longer, stirring occasionally. Serve with French bread. Makes 4 to 6 servings.

SPORTS

Former Blue Jay **Dave Winfield** can pinch hit in oven mitts, too

"I believe that eating right is what has kept me around so long," Dave Winfield says of his 21-year career in the major leagues. "There are certain things you can do to increase your stamina and enhance your performance that begin with good nutrition."

The former Toronto Blue Jay and Minnesota Twins star (now with the Cleveland Indians) is a strong advocate of smart eating. "When you shop for food, read the labels," he advises. "Check the fat and sodium content. In a restaurant, don't be afraid to ask questions about how a dish is prepared."

Winfield's approach to food is an integral part of his philosophy that "health and education are the things you need to make it in life." To that end, he established the New Jersey-based David M. Winfield Foundation in 1977 to help promote health and fitness, including programs on cooking and nutrition counselling.

And though Winfield is better known for wonders worked while wearing a batting glove, he's no slouch in a pair of oven mitts either, as his recipe for Tuna Steak with Green Chili Salsa proves.

TUNA STEAK WITH GREEN CHILI SALSA

2 cups	diced tomatoes	500 mL
1/2 cup	finely chopped onion	125 mL
1	can (about 4 oz/125 mL) mild green chilies, chopped	1
2	jalapeno peppers, minced	2
1/4 cup	fresh lime juice	50 mL
1/4 cup	chopped cilantro	50 mL
2 lbs	tuna steak	1 kg
1/2 cup	olive oil	125 mL
	Red leaf lettuce	
	Freshly ground pepper to taste	

For the salsa, mix together tomatoes, onion, chilies, jalapeno peppers, lime juice and cilantro; set aside for at least 1 hour. Preheat broiler. Brush tuna with olive oil on both sides. Broil tuna for about 5 minutes on each side or until cooked through. Meanwhile, warm salsa in saucepan over low heat for about 5 minutes, stirring constantly. Line plates with lettuce and arrange a portion of tuna on each. Top with warm salsa and black pepper. Makes 4 servings.

SPORTS

Kerrin Lee-Gartner keeps her diet on course with help from her husband

THE ORIGINAL ALBERTA BEEF CRUSTY GRILLED PEPPER STEAKS

6	strip loin steaks (6 oz/175 g each)	6
2	cloves garlic, bruised and peeled	2
1/4 cup	olive oil	50 mL
1/2 cup	cracked or coarsely ground black pepper	125 mL
	Salt	
2 cups	cherry tomatoes	500 mL

Pat steaks dry with paper towel. Rub both sides of each steak with garlic clove, then brush lightly with olive oil. Line large baking sheet with waxed paper. Spread thin layer of pepper on a plate, lightly coat steak with pepper and then place steak on waxed paper. Repeat with remaining steaks and additional pepper. Let stand for 30 minutes in refrigerator. Grill steaks on barbecue until brown and crusty on outside but still pink in centre (5 minutes on each side for medium rare). Garnish with tomatoes. Makes 6 servings.

"For me, race day is the best day in the world," says Canada's Kerrin Lee-Gartner, who won a gold medal in women's downhill at the 1992 Olympics in Albertville.

"When I've got a challenge in front of me, I know it'll take a lot of hard work, luck and, naturally, the right diet," says Lee-Gartner. "I enjoy a lot of carbos the night before a race, especially potatoes and pasta. I also love barbecued meat with a baked potato, and one of my real favorites is my recipe for Crusty Grilled Pepper Steaks which is really quick to prepare."

A 10-year veteran of the ski team, Lee-Gartner also keeps her diet on course with help from her husband and personal coach, Max Gartner. "Max is far more conscious about healthy eating; he helps me keep moderate. The main problem with skiers is that a lot of our program is away from home. I find that if I'm too specific in a diet, it's too hard to follow in all the foreign countries."

SPORTS

John Viehman plans meals ahead for tasty outdoor adventures

Everything tastes much better outdoors," says John Viehman, host of TSN's *Trailside: Make Your Own Adventure*. "You're out there using up a lot of energy, whether it's hiking, climbing or canoeing, and your taste buds say, 'We're going to make a feast of whatever comes our way.'"

Planning meals ahead of time is important for outdoor adventurers. Of course, some food can be caught out there.

"There's nothing better than a fresh fish fry," says Viehman. But he also likes to live it up whenever possible, having enjoyed cheese fondue in the snows of Idaho and key lime pie in the heat of the Everglades. Usually, though, it's necessary to bring food that's either ready to eat or easy to cook with a basic one-burner camp stove.

One staple with Viehman is Missinaibi Energy Bars, which were prepared on a *Trailside* episode about a whitewater canoe expedition on the Missinaibi River northwest of Sault Ste. Marie, Ont. "The cooking times and quantity vary depending on optional ingredients, but it always seems to work," Viehman says. "The bars really taste great, and they do wonders for cranky bow paddlers."

MISSINAIBI ENERGY BAR

4	eggs	4
2 cups	brown sugar	500 mL
1/4 tsp	salt	1 mL
1 tsp	vanilla	5 mL
2 cups	all-purpose flour	500 mL
2 cups	chopped dried fruits (steamed for 10 minutes to soften)	500 mL
1-2 cups	chopped nuts	250-500 mL
1 cup	oats (or any mixture of oats, sesame seeds, sunflower seeds, wheat germ, coconut, etc.)	250 mL

In large saucepan, combine eggs and brown sugar; cook, stirring, over low heat until sugar is dissolved. Add all remaining ingredients. Pat mixture into greased cake pan (about 13 x 9 inches/3.5 L); mixture should not be more than 1 inch/3 cm thick. Bake in 350°F (180°C) oven for 30 to 45 minutes (cooking time varies depending on optional ingredients). Makes about 15 bars.

SPORTS

Debbie Van Kiekebelt makes dinners and workouts a family affair

Former Olympic pentathlete Debbie Van Kiekebelt says, "Keeping up with my kids burns off a lot of energy." But to make sure she stays in shape, "I crank up the stereo and dance around with the kids for a half-hour workout."

At one time, Van Kiekebelt hosted YTV's *Positive Parenting* and although the show gave her great satisfaction, she says that spending time with her husband and two children has always been just as important.

CHICKEN WITH ARTICHOKES

4 to 6	boneless, skinless chicken breasts	4 to 6
1/4 cup	all-purpose flour	50 mL
1/4 cup	butter	50 mL
1-1/2 cups	chicken stock	375 mL
3 tbsp	brandy	50 mL
2 tbsp	lemon juice	25 mL
1 cup	sour cream	250 mL
1	can (14 oz/398 mL) artichoke hearts, drained	1

Coat chicken with half the flour. In skillet, heat half the butter; brown chicken on both sides. Transfer to shallow casserole dish. In same skillet, melt remaining butter and whisk in remaining flour. Gradually add stock, brandy and lemon juice. Stir until sauce thickens, then stir in sour cream (do not boil). Pour over chicken. Bake in 350°F (180°C) oven for 30 minutes. Add artichokes and continue baking for 15 minutes. Serve with rice. Makes 4 to 6 servings.

Some of that time was spent in the kitchen, resulting in one of her dinner party specialties Chicken with Artichokes. "I used to do complicated meals, but now I make simpler meals and get the kids to help."

Sometimes the easiest dinners are one-dish meals, she says, like her family's favorite chili and "other things kids can eat with a spoon. I make a lot of pasta dishes and do stir-fry meals in the wok."

Even though the former athlete manages to set a good nutritional example for her children most of the time, she does admit to a couple of weaknesses: popcorn and dark, dark chocolate.

SPORTS

Hearty fare gives **Elvis Stojko** the lift he needs to dazzle on the ice

MOM'S HOMEMADE BURGERS

1 lb	lean ground beef	500 g
1	egg, lightly beaten	1
1	onion, finely chopped	1
1/3 cup	finely chopped Italian parsley	75 mL
	Salt and freshly ground pepper to taste	
4	hamburger buns, lightly toasted	4

In bowl, combine beef, egg, onion, parsley, salt and pepper. Mix well, using fork or your hands. Shape into 4 patties. Barbecue 4 to 5 minutes on each side. Makes 4 burgers.

When you can perform quadruple jumps and dazzling footwork on ice, possess a black belt in martial arts and have been riding dirt bikes since age seven, you don't have to impress anyone in the kitchen. Besides, in Elvis Stojko's case, there has usually been someone around to do the cooking.

Coming from a European background – his mother is from Hungary, his father from Slovenia – he is used to hearty fare at his Richmond Hill, Ont. home. "My mom makes Hungarian goulash, stuffed peppers, all types of pasta dishes. They give me the energy I need." Having sampled the cuisine at both the Albertville and Lillehammer Olympic villages, he says he found the food in Norway the better of the two. When in doubt, Stojko sticks to his policy of "never eating anything that I don't know before I skate."

Returning to Canada with his silver medal from the '94 Winter Olympics, he looked forward to Mom's Homemade Burgers, which are, as he puts it, "the very best I've ever had."

PHOTO: BROOKE PALMER

SPORTS

Ian Millar sits tall in the saddle thanks to good nutrition

Followers of the equestrian scene know that Canada's Ian Millar is one of the best riders in the world. He's won more than 114 international Grand Prix and derby events and captured two World Cup titles. Though Millar is still a keen competitor, his favorite mount, Big Ben, retired after appearing at the '94 Royal Agricultural Winter Fair in Toronto.

Millar says he's extremely conscious of the need to be at his physical best in competition, and he considers diet to be an important part of his fitness regimen. "Consistency in nutrition seems to work best over the long term for achieving peak stamina and energy," he says. For him, that means eating lean: fresh fruit, vegetables, chicken, salads and eggs.

Between events, he returns home to his farm at Perth, Ont. to regroup with his wife, Lynn, and two children. In summer, Millar enjoys barbecuing at the farm; in frostier weather, he heads inside to prepare heartier fare like this lasagna.

LASAGNA WITH MUSHROOMS

1 lb	lean ground beef	500 g
1	onion, chopped	1
1	clove garlic, minced	1
1 lb	mushrooms, sliced	500 g
1	can (14 oz/398 mL) tomato sauce	1
1 tsp	dried basil	5 mL
1/2 tsp	dried oregano	2 mL
2 tbsp	chopped parsley	25 mL
	Salt and pepper to taste	
2 cups	cottage cheese	500 mL
1 cup	shredded Swiss cheese	250 mL
9	cooked lasagna noodles	9

In large skillet, brown beef with onion and garlic. Add mushrooms and cook until softened. Add tomato sauce, herbs, salt and pepper. Cook until sauce thickens, about 20 minutes. Spread thin layer of sauce over bottom of 12 x 8-inch (3 L) baking pan. Top with a layer of noodles, sauce, cottage cheese and Swiss cheese. Repeat until all ingredients are used up, ending with a layer of noodles topped with a thin layer of sauce and Swiss cheese. Cover pan with foil. Bake in 325°F (160°C) for 1 hour; remove cover for last 15 minutes of baking. Makes 6 servings.

SPORTS

Runner **Charmaine Crooks** listens to her body instead of counting calories

For middle-distance runner Charmaine Crooks – Canada's premiere 800-metre expert and silver medal winner at the '94 Commonwealth Games in Victoria – nutrition is a key component of success. "My body will talk. If I don't treat it carefully, it will react."

At 5-feet-9 and 132 pounds, Crooks doesn't count calories. "I've been running for 15 years and I know what my body needs – veggies, carbs, protein. I also know I can have a piece of chocolate cake. Having a balance is what's important to me."

The middle child in a family of nine, Jamaican-born Crooks credits her parents with tutoring her in healthy eating. "My dad, now 67, still runs and lifts weights." In turn, Crooks has become an example to her husband, Anders Thursen. "My healthy habits have rubbed off on him," she says. "It's a lifestyle I want to maintain well beyond my years as an athlete."

Pasta, chicken and meat are a consistent part of her diet (never seafood because of an allergy). And her coconut-flavored Curry Chicken is first across the finish line every time.

CURRY CHICKEN

4	boneless chicken breasts	4
2 tbsp	olive oil	25 mL
	Salt, pepper, cayenne pepper	
2-3	cloves garlic, crushed	2-3
1	small onion, chopped	1
1	small red bell pepper, julienned	1
2 tbsp	curry powder (or more to taste)	25 mL
1	can (14 oz/398 mL) coconut milk	1
2	potatoes, peeled and chopped	2
1	can (10 oz/284 mL) bamboo shoots	1

Cut chicken into bite-size chunks. In large saucepan, heat oil; add chicken and cook until lightly brown. Add salt, pepper and cayenne pepper to taste. Add garlic, onion and red pepper; cook until softened. Sprinkle in curry powder to taste. Gradually stir in coconut milk. Add potatoes and simmer until tender, about 20 minutes. Add bamboo shoots and simmer for another 3 to 5 minutes. Makes 4 servings.

SPORTS

Michael Jordan's favorite foods take centre court at his restaurant

If the supersized basketball protruding from the restaurant's roof weren't enough, the huge mural of Number 23 soaring through the air would be a certain giveaway that you're in Jordan country: Michael Jordan, former Chicago Bulls basketball superstar and one of the most famous athletes in the world.

While Jordan's dazzling performance is sadly missed at centre court, the man himself is often at the Chicago restaurant that bears his name. Michael Jordan's The Restaurant, which opened in 1993, is just down the street from Oprah Winfrey's The Eccentric.

Chef Peter Heise, who at 6-foot-7 stands one inch taller than the famous hoopster, developed a menu full of Jordan fare, from his traditional pre-game steak and potato to his post-game Crab Cakes to wife Juanita's macaroni and cheese, a Sunday tradition in the Jordan household.

CRAB CAKES

1 lb	lump crabmeat	500 g
1/2 cup	mayonnaise	125 mL
1 tbsp	Worcestershire sauce	15 mL
1 tbsp	Old Bay or other seafood seasoning	15 mL
1 tbsp	chopped parsley	15 mL
1/4 tsp	cayenne pepper	1 mL
Dash	white pepper	Dash
1	large egg	1
1 cup	finely crushed soda crackers	250 mL
1/2 cup	(approx.) vegetable oil or clarified butter for frying	125 mL

Clean any bits of shell from crabmeat. In bowl, combine mayonnaise, Worcestershire sauce, seafood seasoning, parsley, cayenne and white pepper; mix thoroughly. Add egg and cracker crumbs; mix thoroughly. Fold in crabmeat. Taste and add more seasoning if desired. Shape into about 8 patties. In cast iron skillet over medium-high heat, heat oil. Cook crab cakes until golden brown, about 3 minutes on each side. Drain on paper towels. Makes about 4 servings. (Note: This recipe is adapted from Jordan's large-quantity restaurant recipe. The restaurant serves the crab cakes with Mustard Mayonnaise and Lemon-Basil Mayonnaise, garnished with peppers and green onions.)

SPORTS

Broadcaster **Buck Martinez** makes a play for healthy food on the road

For Buck Martinez, TSN's Toronto Blue Jays broadcaster, baseball season means "I kiss my family goodbye in February and say, 'See you in October.'" It also means up to eight months of restaurant and press-box food.

That's why he welcomes a switch to his favorite Oriental Summer Salad when he has a chance to prepare it. "It's a meal in itself. It's light and healthy, something you can make when the weather's hot and you don't feel like eating a lot."

As for trying to eat nutritiously during the long baseball season, Martinez says, "It's not that difficult because restaurants have become more accommodating to the health conscious. But you have to make an effort to not just grab a pizza or hamburger. If I don't keep an eye on what I eat, I gain weight and become lethargic.

"I also didn't realize broadcasting was so demanding from a time aspect," adds Los Angeles-based Martinez, who does baseball coverage for a U.S. cable channel as well as for TSN in Canada. "You keep late hours like when you were a player (he had a 17-year playing career before his seven seasons as a broadcaster), but without all the physical activity. So I work out at hotel gyms and the SkyDome health club when I can."

ORIENTAL SUMMER SALAD

1	package (about 100 g) Ramen or Japanese-style curly noodles with seasoning packet	1
4 cups	shredded cabbage	1 L
4	green onions, chopped	4
2 tbsp	sesame seeds	25 mL
2 tbsp	granulated sugar	25 mL
2 tbsp	vegetable oil	25 mL
1/2 tsp	pepper	2 mL
1-1/2 tsp	salt (or to taste)	7 mL
1/2 cup	slivered almonds	125 mL
	Chopped cooked chicken (optional)	
	Lettuce	

In saucepan of boiling water, cook noodles for about 2 minutes or just until tender but still firm. Drain in colander; rinse with cold water. Mix noodles with cabbage and onions, adding seasoning packet from noodles. Add sesame seeds, sugar, oil, pepper, salt and almonds. Add chopped chicken, if desired. Arrange salad on bed of lettuce. Makes about 4 servings.

MUSIC If music be the food of love, read on

Anne Murray goes back to her roots for traditional Maritime baking

Anne Murray gets a big kick out of being asked for recipes, never mind posing for the cover of a cookbook. "I'm actually not a bad cook, but I prefer to be cooked *for*!"

Murray, who lives most of the year north of Toronto with husband Bill Langstroth and their two teenage children, does in fact tackle cooking, during the summer months at her vacation home in Nova Scotia. "I've cooked many a lobster there in my day," she boasts. However, she points out that her mother, Marion, is the real cook in the family.

The multiple Grammy and Juno winner does admit to more recipe collecting lately, thanks to her daughter, a budding vegetarian. Although Murray was once a physical education teacher, she says she's become even more health conscious in the last 10 years, cutting out a lot of fat in her diet, swimming, playing tennis, golfing and doing aerobics.

Ironically, all this activity has reawakened her sweet tooth. "I went for years without eating sweets at all, but now I think about dessert." That would include this delicious Cherry Cake, a family recipe typical of traditional Maritime baking.

CHERRY CAKE

1-1/2 cups	butter	375 mL
2 cups	granulated sugar	500 mL
4	eggs	4
1 tsp	each: vanilla, almond and lemon extract	5 mL
4 cups	all-purpose flour	1 L
2 tsp	baking powder	10 mL
1 tsp	salt	5 mL
1 cup	milk	250 mL
1-1/2 cups	each: halved red and green candied cherries	375 mL

With electric mixer, cream butter with sugar thoroughly. Add eggs, one at a time, beating well after each. Beat in extracts. Combine 3-1/2 cups (875 mL) of flour with baking powder and salt; mix thoroughly. Add flour mixture to creamed mixture alternately with milk. Toss cherries with remaining 1/2 cup (125 mL) flour; fold into batter. Pour into well-greased and floured 10-inch (3 L) bundt pan. Bake in 325°F (160°C) oven for 1-3/4 hours or until tester inserted in centre comes out clean. Let cool a few minutes in pan, then turn out onto wire rack to cool completely.

MUSIC

Michelle Wright tops the charts but can't beat her mom's pies

With 12 Canadian Country Music Association Awards, Michelle Wright has proven she's no flash in the country music pan. Born in Chatham, Ont., Wright grew up in a musical family and, by her early 20s, was working professionally and traveling with a country band. There were a lot of "just surviving" times, she says, before her hit singles took off on the music charts.

Keeping a band on the road is hard work, but Wright is no stranger to that. "I grew up on a farm and we used to work so hard that, when we got to the dinner table, we'd just eat and eat. My mom's background is Polish, so we had a lot of Eastern European things like cabbage rolls along with meat and vegetables. My mom also made the best pies – rhubarb, apple and rhubarb, and strawberry and rhubarb. I still like to get home for a taste of her homemade pie.

Wright says she and her band try to eat well when they're on the road. "We look for restaurants that serve pasta and salads, and we always have fruit and vegetables and cheese backstage before a concert." At home in Toronto, Wright says, "I love to cook and make a lot of my mom's recipes – especially the pies."

RHUBARB PIE

4 cups	rhubarb (cut in 1-inch/ 3 cm pieces)	1 L
1 tbsp	grated fresh ginger	15 mL
1	egg, beaten	1
	Juice of 1/2 lemon	
1-1/2 cups	granulated sugar	375 mL
3 tbsp	cornstarch	50 mL
2 tbsp	milk	25 mL
	Pastry for double-crust pie (9 inch/23 cm)	

In large bowl, mix together rhubarb, ginger, egg and lemon juice. Mix together sugar and cornstarch; stir into rhubarb mixture. Roll out pastry and fit into 9-inch (23 cm) pie plate. Spoon in filling and top with pastry. Seal and flute edges. Cut a few slashes in top crust and brush with milk. Bake in 425°F (220°C) oven for 15 minutes; reduce heat to 350°F (180°C) and bake for another 40 minutes. Makes about 6 servings.

MUSIC

At Christmas, **Rita MacNeil** makes magic, music and molasses cookies

Much of Rita MacNeil's heartwarming music is a product of her own cherished memories of growing up in Nova Scotia. And none of those memories are more special than the ones associated with Christmases past.

"Our village of Big Pond was a very magical place at Christmastime," says MacNeil who now stars in CBC's *Rita & Friends*. And some of that magic was captured on her TV special, "Once Upon a Christmas," which first aired on CBC in 1993.

The popular Christmas special featured a cozy setting the very picture of a Nova Scotia farmhouse, where the fire crackled and tempting cookies and cranberry punch awaited the first guests.

The set was designed to re-create the heart of MacNeil's grandmother's home – the kitchen. Given that Christmas was always a time for special homemade treats, the kitchen setting was all the more apt. "Molasses Cookies were always a big favorite," recalls MacNeil.

"The recipe has been around for many years, and we also serve them at my Tea Room in Big Pond."

MOLASSES COOKIES

1 cup	shortening	250 mL
1 cup	granulated sugar	250 mL
1 cup	molasses	250 mL
1	egg	1
1 tbsp	baking soda	15 mL
1/2 cup	boiling water	125 mL
4 cups	all-purpose flour	1 L
1 tsp	salt	5 mL
2 tsp	ground ginger	10 mL
2 tsp	ground cloves	10 mL
1 tsp	cinnamon	5 mL

Cream shortening; add sugar gradually, creaming until fluffy. Beat in molasses and egg. Dissolve baking soda in boiling water and add to creamed mixture. Mix together flour, salt, ginger, cloves and cinnamon; add gradually, mixing well to make a soft dough. Chill for at least 30 minutes to make rolling easier. On lightly floured surface, roll dough out to 1/4-inch (5 mm) thickness. Cut into desired shapes. Place on greased baking sheets. Bake in 375°F (190°C) for 8 to 10 minutes. Makes about 6 dozen.

MUSIC

Luciano Pavarotti sings the praises of soccer and pasta

Everybody knows that he can sing, but can Luciano Pavarotti cook? Coincidentally, the world-famous tenor is quite adept in both fields, with full credit going to his father, a professional baker from Modena, Italy.

"I learned to bake [from him]," says Pavarotti. "I worked with him during the summer holidays, and I was always covered with flour. The real difference was that he went to work at 2 in the morning and I didn't begin until 7."

In July, Pavarotti appeared in the hugely successful PBS concert special, "Carreras, Domingo, Pavarotti With Mehta: The Three Tenors in Concert 1994," live from Los Angeles. The concert reunited the men for the first time since their 1990 concert in Rome.

The show also took place on the eve of the World Cup soccer final. When asked which teams he'd like to see in the finals, Pavarotti was diplomatic. "It's not important," he said, smiling, "so long as it is not Italy against Spain. That would be impossible for the concert. All day we talk about the game and do no singing."

In celebration of all good things Italian – whether music, soccer or food – here's some crowd-pleasing, world-class pasta, Pavarotti-style.

SPAGHETTI ALLA CARBONARA

1 to 1-1/4 lbs	medium spaghetti	500 to 625 g
2 tbsp	extra virgin olive oil	25 mL
6 tbsp	unsalted butter, at room temperature	90 mL
8 oz	diced pancetta or prosciutto	250 g
5	eggs	5
	Salt and freshly ground pepper	
3/4 cup	freshly grated Parmesan (preferably Parmigiano Reggiano)	175 mL

In large pot of boiling, lightly salted water, cook pasta al dente (tender but firm). Meanwhile, in skillet, heat oil and melt butter into it. Add pancetta and sauté until dark pink but not crisp. In large serving bowl, beat eggs with a pinch of salt, plenty of pepper and 2 tbsp (25 mL) of Parmesan. Add thoroughly drained hot pasta; toss quickly and thoroughly. Top with pancetta (and a little pan liquid if preferred); toss again. Serve immediately with remaining Parmesan. Makes about 6 servings.

PHOTO: GEORGE LANGE/OUTLINE PRESS

MUSIC

Sharon, Lois and Bram are in harmony when it comes to all kinds of food

Sharon, Lois and Bram love food of all kinds. "We eat everything: falafels, Chinese food, pirogis, blintzes – you name it." All three like to cook, but on the road, "the first thing we do when we hit town is check out the spots where we're going to eat," says Lois.

The singing threesome, familiar to thousands of kids, find that all the traveling and on-location food make staying in shape a tough act. "There's a lot of waiting around," says Sharon, "and there's a tendency to snack." Taking an occasional break at a health spa has helped. "Even after a week, you change a lot of your eating habits."

One of their main dietary discoveries was health-conscious breakfast, which they try to eat as regularly as possible. On weekends, though, the three indulge their shared passion for French toast. An inventive cook, Lois uses croissants and covers them with sour cream or yogurt and fresh berries; Sharon makes hers with English muffins, topped with cottage cheese and strawberry jam; Bram's are on challah (egg bread) topped with marmalade. The trio also agreed on another special treat: Lois's Double Chocolate Brownies.

DOUBLE CHOCOLATE BROWNIES

1 cup	butter	250 mL
1/2 cup	unsweetened cocoa powder	125 mL
4	eggs	4
1-1/4 cups	granulated sugar	300 mL
2 tsp	vanilla	10 mL
1 cup	all-purpose flour	250 mL
1 tsp	baking powder	5 mL
1/2 tsp	salt	2 mL
2 cup	miniature marshmallows	500 mL
1 cup	chocolate chips	250 mL
1 cup	chopped, unsalted peanuts or walnuts	250 mL

In saucepan, melt butter; whisk in cocoa and let cool to room temperature. In large bowl, beat eggs; gradually beat in sugar. Add vanilla; gradually stir in chocolate mixture. Mix together flour, baking powder and salt; stir into batter. Fold in marshmallows, chocolate chips and peanuts. Pour into greased 12 x 8-inch (3 L) cake pan. Bake in 350°F (180°C) oven for 35 to 40 minutes or until top springs back when pressed lightly. Let cool. Dust with icing sugar.

MUSIC

Tarzan Dan Freeman is wild about Italian, Italian and Italian food

Parents, do you know where your children are? Chances are that they're tuned into the madcap antics of YTV's Tarzan Dan and his video countdown show, *The Hit List*.

Freeman got his start in high school where his radio-and-television-arts teacher warned him that he was "nuts, crazy, kinda weird, and if I got into radio, most people would think I'm normal," he says. His pro career took him to Calgary where he became the "voice of the 1988 Winter Olympics for CFCN and CTV." Calgary is also where his moniker, Tarzan Dan, was coined.

Friends were kidding him about the untamed jungle-like feel of his show. "I remember thinking, 'What's in a jungle?' And someone said 'Tarzan. Yeah, Tarzan Dan!' It's stuck with me since."

MARINATED MUSHROOMS

3/4 lb	small mushrooms	375 g
1/2 cup	olive oil	125 mL
1/4 cup	white wine vinegar	50 mL
1	clove garlic, minced	1
1	small onion, minced	1
1/2 tsp	oregano, crumbled	2 mL
Dash	crushed red pepper	Dash
	Salt and pepper to taste	

Rinse mushrooms gently under cold water; drain well on paper towels. In large bowl, combine remaining ingredients. Add mushrooms and stir to coat. Cover and chill for at least 2 hours. Makes about 4 servings.

He says he always enjoyed having his own radio show "but to get my own video show is, wow, the coolest thing." His hectic schedule leaves little time for cooking, so it's a good thing his tastes are simple: "Italian, Italian, Italian and lobster," and for dessert, "chocolate and hockey. I'm a Canucks fan."

Freeman says he's "not into the meat thing any more. I used to think, 'Wow, steak!' Now I prefer fish and vegetables." He serves his Marinated Mushrooms with grilled swordfish steaks that he brushes with a marinade of lime juice, olive oil and black pepper, and that he describes in his typical understated manner: "Amazing!"

MUSIC

Crash Test Dummies' Ellen Reid plays it smart about her food

GRILLED SWORDFISH

4	swordfish steaks (4 oz/125 g each)	4
2 tbsp	olive oil	25 mL
3 tbsp	lemon juice	50 mL
1 tbsp	dry sherry	15 mL
2 tsp	soy sauce	10 mL
2	cloves garlic, minced	2
1 tbsp	minced fresh ginger	15 mL
1 tbsp	grated lemon rind	15 mL

Place swordfish steaks in shallow pan. Combine remaining ingredients to make marinade. Pour over fish and turn to coat. Cover and refrigerate for 2 hours. On barbecue grill or in skillet lightly coated with olive oil, cook swordfish just until cooked through, about 5 to 6 minutes per side. Makes 4 servings.

After appearing on every TV talk show under the sun, Winnipeg's Crash Test Dummies have a pretty clear fix as to who puts on the best pre-show spread. "So far, we've done *Arsenio, Letterman, Saturday Night Live, Conan O'Brien* and *Jay Leno*," says keyboardist-vocalist Ellen Reid, "and, so far, *Arsenio* had the best spread.

"There was a big fruit plate, tons of vegetables, fresh bread, salads and some hot food, too. It was pretty impressive."

What made it especially impressive, says Reid, was that it recognized the group's collective approach to nutrition. "Every one of us is very conscious of healthy eating these day," she says. "No eating big bags of M&Ms every night."

Recently, they toured with Elvis Costello – which meant further fine dining. And since they ate out almost every night, when she gets home to Winnipeg, Reid says she loves to entertain. She often prepares a simple summer dish like tabbouleh or her Grilled Swordfish. But if the Dummies' tour schedule ever gears down, Reid plans on getting *truly* serious. "I *love* to cook. I'm going to enrol in cooking school."

PERMISSIONS

P. 4 From "In the Kitchen with Rosie" by Rosie Daley. Copyright © 1994 by Rosie Daley. Reprinted by permission of Alfred A. Knopf, Inc.

P. 10 From "Cooking with Regis & Kathie Lee" by Regis Philbin and Kathie Lee Gifford with Barbara Albright. Copyright © 1993 by Regis Philbin and Kathie Lee Gifford with Barbara Albright. Reprinted by permission of Hyperion.

P. 15 From "The Lifestyles of the Rich and Famous Cookbook" by Robin Leach. Copyright © 1992 by Television Program Enterprises, Inc. Reprinted by permission of Viking Penguin, a division of Penguin Books USA, Inc.

P. 22 From "Entertaining with Regis & Kathie Lee" by Regis Philbin and Kathie Lee Gifford with Barbara Albright. Copyright © 1994 by Regis Philbin and Kathie Lee Gifford with Barbara Albright. Reprinted by permission of Hyperion.

P. 42 From "The High Road to Health" by Lindsay Wagner and Ariane Spade. Copyright © 1990 by Lindsay Wagner and Ariane Spade. Reprinted by permission of Simon & Schuster, Inc.

P. 52 From "The Anne of Green Gables Cookbook" by Kate Macdonald. Copyright © 1985. Reprinted by permission of Kate Macdonald and Oxford University Press Canada.

P. 64 From "The Northern Exposure Cookbook" by Ellis Weiner, based on the Universal Television series created by Joshua Brand and John Falsey. Copyright © 1993 by MCA Publishing Rights, a Division of MCA Inc. Used with permission of Contemporary Books, Chicago.

P. 85 Reprinted with permission of Newsstand Publications and "The Official Coronation Street Magazine," 1994.

P. 92 Adapted from a recipe from "The Well-Seasoned Wok," 1993. Published by Harlow & Ratner. Reprinted by permission of Martin Yan.

P. 94 From "The Way to Cook" by Julia Child. Copyright © 1989 by Julia Child. Reprinted by permission of Alfred A. Knopf, Inc.

P. 95 From "Simply HeartSmart Cooking" by The Heart and Stroke Foundation of Canada and Bonnie Stern's Cooking Schools Ltd. Copyright © 1994. Reprinted by permission of Random House.

P. 97 From "Pam's Kitchen" by Pam Collacott. Copyright © 1990 by Pam Collacott. Reprinted with permission of Macmillan Canada, a division of Canada Publishing Corp.

P. 98 From "Death by Chocolate" by Marcel Desaulniers. Copyright © 1992 by Marcel Desaulniers. Reprinted by permission of Random House.

P. 99 From "Eating Well" by Burt Wolf. Copyright © 1992 by Burt Wolf. Reprinted with permission of Doubleday Canada, Ltd.

P. 102 From "Tiger in the Kitchen: Done Like Dinner" by Tiger Williams and Kasey Wilson. Copyright © 1987. Reprinted by permission of Douglas & McIntyre.

P. 120 From "The Authentic Pasta Cookbook" by Fred Plotkin. Copyright © 1985 by Fred Plotkin. Reprinted by permission of Simon & Schuster, Inc.

CELEBRITY INDEX
Aprea, John, 87
Ashford, Matthew, 88
Baker, Kathy, 49
Barber, James, 101
Bosley, Tom, 65
Botsford, Sara, 41
Byrnes, Jim, 44
Cheers: Bull & Finch Pub, 79
Cherry, Don, 105
Child, Julia, 94
Christopher, Thom, 91
Clark, Dick, 19
Collacott, Pam, 97
Crash Test Dummies, 124
Crooks, Charmaine, 112
Dale, Cynthia, 40
Deol, Monika, 25
Desaulniers, Marcel, 98
Driver, Betty, 85
Eakes, Bobbie, 84
Ephron, Nora, 50
Ferguson, Don, 72
Flaherty, Joe, 75
Fulton, Eileen, 90
Gifford, Kathie Lee, 10
Gilmour, David, 13
Grad, Laurie Burrows, 100
Gretzky, Wayne, 104
Hanomansing, Ian, 36
Jackson, Tom, 53
Jennings, Lynette, 24
Jones, Jenny, 9
Jordan, Michael, 114
Lansbury, Angela, 38
Leach, Robin, 15
Lee-Gartner, Kerrin, 107
Lewis, Shari, 12
Light, Judith, 68
Lucci, Susan, 86
MacLean, Ron, 102
MacNeil, Rita, 119
Malling, Eric, 21
Marin, Cheech, 62
Martinez, Buck, 115
Matheson, Don, 30
Mesley, Wendy, 33
Millar, Ian, 111
Mills, Alley, 69
Murray, Anne, 116
Myers, Mike, 71
Nash, Knowlton, 28
Newhart, Bob, 70
Northern Exposure, 64
Pavarotti, Luciano, 120
Petty, Dini, 8
Philbin, Regis, 22
Polley, Sarah, 52
Potter, Carol, 43
Potter, Chris, 56
Pringle, Valerie, 31
Regalbuto, Joe, 78
Rinaldo, Sandie, 32
Rivera, Geraldo, 7
Roseanne, 66
Rostad, Wayne, 18
Rowell, Victoria, 82
Saldana, Theresa, 48
Schull, Rebecca, 80
Scully, Robert, 20
Seinfeld: Tom's Restaurant, 58
Sharon, Lois & Bram, 122
Shatner, William, 47
Simmons, Richard, 26
The Simpsons, 61
Smith, Alison, 34
Smith, Steve, 63
Solomon, Shirley, 6
Stern, Bonnie, 95
Stewart, Martha, 96
Stojko, Elvis, 110
Stone, Pam, 76
"Tarzan Dan" Freeman, 123
Taylor, Meshach, 74
Tesh, John, 16
Thicke, Alan, 60
Trebek, Alex, 14
Tucker, Michael, 54
Van Kiekebelt, Debbie, 109
Viehman, John, 108
Visitor, Nana, 46
Wagner, Lindsay, 42
Wallin, Pamela, 37
Weathers, Carl, 55
Winfield, Dave, 106
Winfrey, Oprah, 4
Wolf, Burt, 99
Wright, Michelle, 118
Yan, Martin, 92

RECIPE INDEX
Animal Salads, 97
Appetizers and Snacks:
    Fireside Fondue, 86
    Jalapeno Corn Fritters, 44
    Lobster Dip, 69
    Missinaibi Energy Bars, 108
    Mozzarella Marinara, 12
    Parc Montsouris, 20
    Ricotta Bruschetta, 95
    Sour Cream Cucumber Dip, 55
    Theresa Pizza, 48
Apple Crisp, 49
Apple Fritters, 71
Asian Burgers, 92
Baked Easter Ham, 96
Banana-Nut Bread, 47
Bannock, 53
Barbecue Chicken, 70
Barbecued Butterflied Leg of Lamb, 31
Beef: see Meats
Beef Machaca, 62
Boneless Stuffed Turkey, 72
Breaded Pork Chops, 61
Breads:
    Banana-Nut Bread, 47
    Bannock, 53
    Carrot-Bran Muffins, 9
    Cornbread, 90
    Good Day Pancakes, 43
    Peasant Picnic Loaf, 54
    Power Loaf, 38
    Ricotta Bruschetta, 95
Cabbage Borscht, 80
Cabbage Rolls, 6
Cakes: see Desserts
Cajun Corn Chowder, 19
Cajun-Creole Shrimp, 74
Carrot-Bran Muffins, 9
Cherry Cake, 116
Cherry's Chili, 105
Chicken:
    with Artichokes, 109
    Barbecue, 70
    Biryani, 25
    Coconut, 36
    Curry, 112
    Light Mustard, 68
    Ragout, Garlic, 13
    Rich and Famous, 15
    Un-Fried, 4
Chicken Biryani, 25
Chicken with Artichokes, 109
Chili, Cherry's, 105
Chocolate-Dipped Strawberries, 32
Chocolate Mousse, 94
Chocolate Turtle Squares, 24
Cioppino, 66
Cocktail, Devil's Advocate, 20
Coconut Chicken, 36
Cookies and Squares:
    Chocolate Turtle Squares, 24
    Double Chocolate Brownies, 122
    Missinaibi Energy Bars, 108
    Molasses Cookies, 119
Cornbread, 90
Corned Beef and Cabbage, 79
Coronation Street Hotpot, 85
Crab Cakes, 114
Crusty Grilled Pepper Steaks, 107
Cumin Noodles, 64
Curry Chicken, 112
Desserts:
    Apple Crisp, 49
    Apple Fritters, 71
    Cherry Cake, 116
    Chocolate-Dipped Strawberries, 32
    Chocolate Mousse, 94
    Chocolate Turtle Squares, 2⁄
    Double Chocolate Browni⸱

Georgia Pecan Pie, 84
Key Lime Pie, 60
Marilla's Plum Pudding, 52
Mocha Java Sorbet, 98
Molasses Cookies, 119
Out-of-this-World Gingerbread, 46
Pumpkin Cheesecake, 22
Raspberry Mousse Pie, 33
Rhubarb Pie, 118
Rich Rum Pie, 40
Tiramisu, 50
Devil's Advocate Cocktail, 20
Double Chocolate Brownies, 122
Eggs:
  Eggs Goldenrod, 8
  Parc Montsouris, 20
  Turkey and Cheese Omelette, 37
Eggs Goldenrod, 8
Fillet of Sole or Grouper with Lime and Almonds, 28
Fireside Fondue, 86
Fish Chowder, 34
Fish and Seafood:
  Cajun-Creole Shrimp, 74
  Cioppino, 66
  Crab Cakes, 114
  Fillet of Sole or Grouper with Lime and Almonds, 28
  Fish Chowder, 34
  Grilled Swordfish, 124
  Lobster Dip, 69
  Seafood Shish Kebabs, 10
  Steamed Salmon, 82
  Tuna Steak with Green Chili Salsa, 106
Fluffy Light Meat Loaf, 100
Fondue, Fireside, 86
Garlic Chicken Ragout, 13
Georgia Pecan Pie, 84
Good Day Pancakes, 43
Goulash, Rostad, 18
Gretzky's Great Pirogis, 104
Grilled Pork Tenderloin, 63
Grilled Swordfish, 124
Grouper with Lime and Almonds, 28
Hot Pepper Soup, 41
Italian Sausage Pasta, 102
Jalapeno Corn Fritters, 44
Key Lime Pie, 60
Lamb: see Meats
Lamb Shish Kebabs, 58
Lasagna with Mushrooms, 111
Latkes (Potato Pancakes), 7
Light Mustard Chicken, 68
Linguine with Red Clam Sauce, 65
Linguine with Pesto, 78
Lobster Dip, 69
Marilla's Plum Pudding, 52

Marinated Mushrooms, 123
Meatballs, Swedish, 21
Meat Loaf, Fluffly Light, 100
Meat Pies, 99
Meats:
  Asian Burgers, 92
  Baked Easter Ham, 96
  Barbecued Butterflied Leg of Lamb, 31
  Beef Machaca, 62
  Breaded Pork Chops, 61
  Cabbage Rolls, 6
  Cherry's Chili, 105
  Corned Beef and Cabbage, 79
  Coronation Street Hotpot, 85
  Crusty Grilled Pepper Steaks, 107
  Fluffy Light Meat Loaf, 100
  Grilled Pork Tenderloin, 63
  Lamb Shish Kebabs, 58
  Meat Pies, 99
  Mom's Homemade Burgers, 110
  Pocket Pork Chops, 26
  Rostad Goulash, 18
  Swedish Meatballs, 21
  Teriyaki Flank Steak, 30
  Tourtière Trebek, 14
Minestrone Soup, 56
Missinaibi Energy Bars, 108
Mocha Java Sorbet, 98
Molasses Cookies, 119
Mom's Homemade Burgers, 110
Mozzarella Marinara, 12
Muffins, Carrot-Bran, 9
Mushrooms:
  Marinated, 123
  Stuffed, 88
Oriental Summer Salad, 115
Original Alberta Beef Crusty Grilled Pepper Steaks, 107
Out-of-this-World Gingerbread, 46
Pancakes, Good Day, 43
Parc Montsouris, 20
Pasta:
  Cumin Noodles, 64
  Italian Sausage Pasta, 102
  Lasagna with Mushrooms, 111
  Linguine with Red Clam Sauce, 65
  Linguine with Pesto, 78
  Pasta Sorrento, 87
  Pennoni al Tonno, 75
  Spaghetti alla Carbonara, 120
Pasta Sorrento, 87
Peasant Picnic Loaf, 54
Pennoni al Tonno, 75
Pies: see Desserts
Pirogis, Gretzky's Great, 104
Pizza, Theresa, 48
Pocket Pork Chops, 25
Pork: see Meats

Potato Pancakes (Latkes), 7
Power Loaf, 38
Pumpkin Cheesecake, 22
Raspberry Mousse Pie, 33
Red and Yellow Pepper Stew with Anchovies, 101
Rhubarb Pie, 118
Rich Rum Pie, 40
Rich and Famous Chicken, 15
Ricotta Bruschetta, 95
Rostad Goulash, 18
Salads:
  Bunny, Mousey, Spider, 97
  Oriental Summer Salad, 115
  Tabbouleh Salad, 42
Saskatoon Berry Soup, 53
Seafood: see Fish and Seafood
Seafood Shish Kebabs, 10
Snacks: see Appetizers and Snacks
Sole with Lime and Almonds, 28
Soups:
  Cabbage Borscht, 80
  Cajun Corn Chowder, 19
  Fish Chowder, 34
  Hot Pepper Soup, 41
  Minestrone Soup, 56
  Saskatoon Berry Soup, 53
Sour Cream Cucumber Dip, 55
Spaghetti alla Carbonara, 120
Squares: see Cookies and Squares
Steaks: see Meats
Steamed Salmon, 82
Stuffed Mushrooms, 88
Stuffed Peppers with Eggplant and Feta Cheese, 16
Swedish Meatballs, 21
Tabbouleh Salad, 42
Teriyaki Flank Steak, 30
Theresa Pizza, 48
Tiramisu, 50
Tourtière Trebek, 14
Tuna Steak with Green Chili Salsa, 106
Turkey:
  Boneless Stuffed Turkey, 72
  Turkey and Cheese Omelette, 37
Un-Fried Chicken, 4
Vegetables:
  Cabbage Rolls, 6
  Jalapeno Corn Fritters, 44
  Potato Pancakes (Latkes), 7
  Red and Yellow Pepper Stew with Anchovies, 101
  Stuffed Peppers with Eggplant and Feta Cheese, 16
  Wok Vegetables, 91
  Zucchini and Corn Casserole, 76
Wok Vegetables, 91
Zucchini and Corn Casserole, 76